First published in 2020 by Streetlight Publishing.

INTRODUCTION

Somewhere, somehow, during 2019 a strain of coronavirus perked up and announced itself to the world. We all know what happened next, and in March 2020 the UK went into lockdown. A couple of years ago I had written a book, Cycling Down the Street, (which is quite marvellous, by the way - you would love it, so don't hesitate to buy it) and had wondered ever since what to do as a follow-up. But every cloud, as they say, has a silver lining, and it was clear that I would have to do something useful during lockdown to distract me from thoughts of murdering my three teenage boys. I thought, too, that if I couldn't find something interesting and amusing to say about the extraordinary events that were unfolding, then I really should give up trying to write anything ever again. So, lo and behold, three months later this book came blinking and staggering out of lockdown with the rest of us. I hope it makes you smile in places, and maybe pause for thought in others. But, in any event, my sons are still unmurdered - so I guess it was definitely worthwhile writing for that reason alone. Well, probably.

DEDICATION

This book was written under trying circumstances. At least that is what my family told me, as they were trying very hard to put up with me even more than usual. So, thank you Edina, Rafi, Jamie and Anthony for your patience. Thank you too to everyone who followed the Wuhan Diaries on Facebook, and in particular to my good friends Brendan and Austin, for their support and dedication to their daily read.

ROVER'S

CYCLING DOWN THE STREET

Three thousand miles on a bike is a long way at the best of times. Particularly on your own. So, when you are riding your bike - and its enormous amount of luggage - very slowly up and down the hills of five countries, there is plenty of time to think. Which Coronation Street character last night's hotel most called to mind, for instance. Not what you'd normally expect to find in a travel blog, granted, but this isn't a normal travel blog. In equal measure it's hilarious and thought-provoking - and you get to meet Peter's intriguing friends who pop up every now and then to lend him some support. Luis, a man for whom sleaze is just the Vaseline that helps him slide out of bed each morning. Brendan, who once pulled up in a 400m race with a displaced male appendage. And Jeff, who leaves no seduction stone unturned in his eternal quest for female conquest. Cycling Down The Street is a great read - unless you happen to be a Manchester United fan, of course, when you are strongly advised not to buy this book.

"I really enjoyed your book. What a great idea, relating things to Street characters, it is a wonderful way of conveying the feeling and atmosphere of the place. Very readable, very enjoyable and very informative. Hope the book does really well and here's to the next."

William Roach (Ken Barlow)

"It is truly brilliant, and a great mixture of philosophy, near-death experiences, travel reports, focus on food, laugh out loud moments and even a bit of Coronation Street thrown in for those of us of a Northern disposition. Well done on your achievement - I'm looking forward to the next trip already!"

Lesley Munroe-Faure

THE WUHAN DIARIES

CONTENTS

22ND MARCH - THE DONALD

Now, some of the more politically correct amongst you might think that there are overtones of racism in the title of my blog. That, by referencing the origin of the pandemic, (that's Wuhan, for the less news-savvy) I am casting blame upon that fine city that none of us had ever heard of just three months ago. Or that, in drawing attention to their predilection for munching live bats and making soup of their entrails, I am, in some small way, allocating blame to the Wuhanese for this global pandemic that has brought the world to a standstill, and (temporarily) halted Liverpool's inexorable charge to a glorious and record breaking premier league title. Nothing could be further from the truth. I am relatively sure that the good people of Wuhan are no less lovely, nor more disgusting, than those anywhere else in China. And you can't say fairer than that, can you? If you're looking for a man casting blame, however, you need look no further than the President of the United States of America. Donald Trump, as many of you will have spotted, is very keen indeed to call this the 'Chinese Virus'. Which is all wrong really, since I am guessing the virus is possessed of very few obviously Chinese traits. It almost certainly doesn't eat with chopsticks, nor drown its offspring when it finds out they are girls. No, I think it's fair to say that Coronavirus is a citizen of the world, and its ability to settle into different communities, irrespective or creed or colour, is actually quite impressive in its own way.

Trump, however, would not have you see the world this way. It suits his agenda to personify this faceless threat with Chinese characteristics, in the same way that we painted all German soldiers in the first world war as baby killers and nun-rapists. By creating a backdrop, where the subtext is that China is to blame, it deflects attention away from his own spectacularly inept approach to the growing crisis. Mind you, Trump has good company - the Chinese themselves are responding to the challenge of the blame game with some gusto. After an initial stab at putting the blame for the emergence of the virus on the US military, they have been much cheered that there are now more deaths in Europe than China, and have been pushing the idea that it didn't originate in China at all. It would all be quite entertainingly childish were these not two of the world superpowers. The Americans still have over six thousand nuclear weapons, after all. Only the Russians are capable of greater nuclear devastation, which is a cheering thought - particularly as they have now perfected an underwater nuke designed to swamp cities with radioactive tsunamis. And to think we're getting all hot and bothered about a bit of a virus!

Anyhow, on a less cataclysmic note, back to The Donald. Alarming and dangerous though he is, in a slightly gallows' humour kind of way it is quite entertaining to listen to the nonsense he sprouts. Here is a timeline to some of his pronouncements so far:

January 22nd	'We have it totally under control. It's one person coming in from China, and we have it under control. It's going to be just fine.'
January 30th	'We think we have it very well under control. We have very little problem in this country at this moment - five - and those people are all recuperating successfully. But we're working very closely with China and other countries, and we think it's going to have a very good ending for us.'
February 10th	'Now, the virus that we're talking about having to do - you know, a lot of people think that goes away in April with the heat, as the heat comes in. Typically, that will go away in April. We're in great shape, though. We have 12 cases, 11 cases, and many of them are in good shape now.'
February 26th	'We're going to be pretty soon at only five people. And we could be at just one or two people over the next short period of time. So, we've had very good luck.'
February 27th	'It's going to disappear. One day - it's like a miracle - it will disappear.'

March 4th	Trump calls the WHO's estimate of the global death rate 'false', describes the coronavirus as 'very mild', and suggests that those infected can get better by 'sitting around' and 'going to work'.
March 7th	'No, I'm not concerned at all. No, I'm not. No, we've done a great job.'
March 9th	'The Fake News Media and their partner, the Democrat Party, is doing everything within its semi-considerable power (it used to be greater!) to inflame the coronavirus situation, far beyond what the facts would warrant. The risk is low to the average American. So last year thirty-seven thousand Americans died from the common Flu. It averages between twenty-seven thousand and seventy thousand per year. Nothing is shut down, life & the economy go on. At this moment there are five hundred and forty-six confirmed cases of coronavirus, with twenty-two deaths. Think about that!'

Think about that indeed! It is hard to imagine anything more deluded outside of a Manchester United Board Meeting. But, here's a prediction for you. When this is all over, and there are tens of thousands of dead Americans, my money will be on one man taking all the credit for it having finally ended. No matter how bloody hot it gets in April!

23RD MARCH - THE PREDICTION GAME

In times of uncertainty, everyone looks to the future - and it appears that there is much capital to be gained in the prediction business. There is a whole industry surrounding Nostradamus, and in interpreting his astonishingly vague portents in mind-bendingly ridiculous ways. Consider this for instance:

The great plague of the city
Will not cease until there be avenged the death
Of the just blood, condemned for a price without crime
Of the great lady outraged by pretense
Brothers and sisters captive in diverse places

According to received wisdom in predicting circles this is, apparently, supposed to mean that, 'A serious illness will attack a maritime city, and that the epidemic will spread to many countries around the world, and people will no longer be able to travel.' Well, if for the time being we ignore the fact that Wuhan is seven hundred kilometres inland, I'm still not sure I would immediately jump to thinking, 'Worldwide pandemic!' from that particular quatrain. It's much the same thing with Dean Koontz, who some people seem to now think predicted the current outbreak because his novel, *The Eyes of Darkness*, contains the word *Wuhan-400*. I ask you! But it got me thinking. There is most definitely fame and fortune to be gained from being thought a prophet - particularly when people are looking for hope. And I think I might just have what it takes to make it in the Prediction Game; my credentials are impeccable - when Edina was pregnant, for instance, I correctly predicted she was having a baby. So, with such an impeccable track record, why shouldn't I have a crack at this future-telling caper?

The normal scam, from what I can glean, is to make as many nebulous predictions as possible, in as lofty a tone as possible, in the hope that one of them might, in hindsight, be interpretable as foretelling a seismic event. Well, I'm going to buck half of this trend. I'm going to give you the first twenty of my prescient insights, yes, but they are going to be bang on the money, rather than irritatingly cryptic. Predictions so precise, so sharp, that you could circumcise a virus with them! If just one of them hits strikes golddirt I will be hailed a genius, and you will be able to dine out for years on your perspicacity at being an early stage liker of my Facebook page. So, here goes:

1. The divorce rate in London in 2021 will increase by thirty-four per cent compared with 2019.

2. By a factor of three, more children will be born in the UK on Christmas day this year than on any other Christmas day in history.

3. No one in the whole world will name their daughter 'Corona' in 2020. (How ironic, though, that 'Corona' is an Italian name as Italy is now covid-central - '*ti amo Corona*' is never going to sound the same again!). Though, incredibly, some people will name their child 'Donald' = particularly as it shows early signs of being a complete prick.

4. The Dow Jones index will be exactly the same on 12th February 2021 as it was on 12th February 2020.

5. More than twice as many people will die of the virus in Iran than in any other country. Not many of us in the West will give a toss.

6. Prince Andrew will be arrested in April, extradited to the US, and tried on a fast-track with great fanfare. Mainly so as we can have some diversionary reality television to take our minds off horrible grubby little things we can't see, and replace them with horrible grubby things we can see. Huge sums of money will trade on the timing of the first bead of sweat we see on the royal forehead.

7. There will be a twenty-nine per cent increase in the birth-rate in the UK in first quarter of 2021 compared to the first quarter of this year. The most popular boys' name will be Rishi. Coincidentally, the most popular girls' name will be Rishi too, which will make naming twins a minefield.

8. One of my boys will accidentally discover an antidote to the virus during his direct learning biology lesson. Regrettably, he will forget to save his formula, which will then be lost when we have a power-cut. As a consequence, many people who otherwise might have

been saved will get to join the ventilator queue. He will think it is unreasonable that I tick him off for this.

9. Donald Trump will, incredibly, win the 2020 presidential election; garnering fifty-three per cent of the vote.

10. Meghan Markle will be discovered to have self-injected the virus in order to improve her popularity ratings - only to find that people dislike the new disease-ridden Meghan even more than the normal smug one.

11. The basic rate of income tax will increase by three pence in next year's budget. The man in the street will think this is outrageous, and that the additional four trillion pounds of public debt should be funded entirely from a mansion tax on people who live in South Oxfordshire.

12. On 12th April someone in Newcastle will be beaten to death for drinking Corona lager in the park. His ashes will be spread over St James' Park, together with a slice of lime and the crumbs from his bag of salt and vinegar.

13. The US investment in military and weapons will increase to more than fifty-four cents in every tax dollar. Most elements of their defence budget with remain static, but the biggest increase will be on research in biological warfare.

14. Court Farm Barn B&B bookings will be down fifty-eight per cent on the year. Though, incredibly, my wife will still contrive to keep the heating on full-blast over the whole time.

15. One of my boys will be accused of knocking up someone's daughter, but I will be able to plausibly deny it on the basis he never left the house.

16. A horse named *Catch Me If You Can* will win the two o'clock race at Kempton on 20th September 2020.

17. On the day the lockdown is ended, there will be exactly the same number of people admitted to the London hospitals for alcohol poisoning as were admitted for viral infection on 18st March. It will become known as *Grey Goose Day*, and will be a public holiday in future years.

18. Liverpool will win the EPL in front of a crowd of seventeen spectators, and a worldwide TV audience of over a billion. Manchester United will fail to qualify for the Champions League, and will approach Donald Trump to replace Ole Gunar Solsjaer. Trump will take United into the Championship, and then announce he has done a 'beautiful job', and that losing seven-one at home to Everton was just 'fake news.' Most people are inclined to believe him on this last one.

19. Maria Sharapova will tragically fall victim to Coronavirus, and we will discover that she contracted it by handling far too many balls when she was supposed to be self-isolating. She will win the BBC Sportsperson of the Year award for the loudest recorded grunting in A&E.

20. Boris Johnson will physically explode. It will become the most watched YouTube video of all time.

Should any of you actually bet on any of this - particularly on Boris exploding, where I understand odds have drifted out to a tasty fifteen to two on BET365 - can I just remind you that a 'Nostradamus fee' of fifteen per cent is traditionally payable to the Predictor out of your net winnings. Happy betting, but always remember people - Gamble Aware. And when the fun stops, stop!

24TH MARCH - ON EXPERTS AND POLITICIANS

There is nothing quite like a crisis. It's like springtime for experts and wannabe-experts, they pop out of the woodwork like tortoises in the sunshine. Not that tortoises live in woodwork, but you get my gist. Whilst all wannabe-experts, by definition really, like to pass themselves off as the real thing, it's actually quite easy to tell the one from the other - even when they are saying exactly the same thing. The wannabe-expert is insufferably smug as he relishes his moment in the sun, secure in the knowledge that he doesn't actually have to take responsibility for the consequences of his opinions. The actual expert, has a completely different persona. He typically looks and sounds considerably more worried: partly because he is probably in possession of more worrying facts than the rest of us, and partly, I imagine, because he has the pressure of knowing that his advice may well have very real and devastating consequences.

Which brings me onto politicians. In a world of wannabe experts, these boys are the Premier League players. At the best of times the majority are self-congratulatory wankers, who have only a passing inkling of the distain with which most of us hold them, and the parliamentary process which they infest like wriggling maggots on a dead cat. But crises are when they puff up their feathers even more, when they really believe they MATTER. When it's business as usual, with nothing critical on the agenda, they comfort themselves that they can be 'good constituency MPs'. But we all know they hate this really; that they yearn to wander in and out of the House against a backdrop of microphones and cameras which illuminate their relevance to the big issue of the day. Crises are their existential moments - where they can feel that they are at the centre of things, where can beat their chests and sound worthy and profound amidst an orgy of sanctimony. Brexit was perfect for this. They could all profess great insight, they could take sides and masterdebate their little hearts out.

But there is a really interesting paradox which comes into play, I'm coming to come to realise. I am calling it the *Crisis Bell Curve*, and let me try and explain it. Imagine a graph, where the X-axis measures the severity of a crisis, and the Y-axis denotes the stiffness of a parliamentarian's manhood in response to that crisis. (I'm not trying to be sexist here, there is clearly a female equivalent, I'm just not inclined to write about it if I'm honest). Now, as we move along the X-axis, and the scale of the crisis intensifies, the parliamentary stiffy snaps to attention. You can almost smell the testosterone pulsating through those rampant egos. And the further we go along the X-axis, the greater the stiffiness on the Y axis. Until it reaches a peak - normally just around the point in the crisis where what we need is some bloody leadership; someone to make some decisions, rather than a bunch of schoolchildren debating in the assembly hall. And, as we move ever further along the X-axis, as the crisis morphs into a national emergency, the more parliamentarian flaccidity sets in. And, for the average MP, this becomes a personal existential crisis all of its own. They are impotent and have nothing to do. Arguably they never did, but now it's clear everyone that, while the top bods are locked away doing the macho stuff, they're sat at home being about as useful as Anne Frank's drum kit.

What brought all this to mind? Well I don't do Twitter much, but the boys' schools both have Twitter feeds, so every now and then I have a quick look. Oddly, there was a tweet yesterday from an MP called Lucy Powell in Manchester, who had posted some photos of an empty park captioned *Our local park in Manchester at 10am. Just to counter the narratives* ... Now, I've never actually tweeted before, but I was moved too because I bloody hate people who talk about 'narrative'. So I tweeted her back. I suggested that the reason that the park was empty was probably because it was Monday morning - and not the weekend. Well, blow me if she didn't get right back to me and tell me that, not only was the park empty, but the roads and Manchester City centre were very quiet too. Clearly a woman with time on her hands. I politely pointed out to her that the roads were almost certainly quiet because lots of people were working at home - as the government had advised. Though I did resist the temptation to tell her that Manchester city centre was empty because it was a shithole. I'm tactful like that. Anyway, I looked at her tweet history later in the day, and while I'm sure Lucy is a lovely, well-intentioned lady, judging by the volume and content of her tweets, what is completely clear is that she has no meaningful job right now;

no idea of what her purpose should be at this critical moment in time. I was almost starting to feel sorry for her until I read a reply she had written to a tweet of another MP, Matthew Pennycook. I will give you Matthew's tweet first, then her response:

Matthew: *It's crucial that each and every one of us, including MPs, plays our part in slowing the spread of COVID19 and for that reason I've decided, after much thought, not to travel to Westminster today to debate the COVID19 emergency legislation.*

Lucy: *Same here. Travelling down from Manchester is unthinkable. These are challenging times and we need to take our own responsibilities to public health seriously.*

Which could quite easily be paraphrased:

Matthew *I've got bugger all to say, and no-one's going to listen anyhow, so I'm going to stay home and watch Peaky Blinders.*

Lucy. *Yeah, can't be arsed either really as no-one wants to listen to me. Think I'll go online and sent pointless tweets - so my fanny doesn't dry up completely before we have that that billionth debate on House of Lords reform in the Autumn.*

Anyhow, you've probably heard enough by now of my views of the average parliamentarian. My apologies to Lucy (but not to Matthew, who sounds a frightful arse) and I will leave you with one final comment. In an interview on Sunday, the current leader of Her Majesty's opposition explained that, ten years ago, he had had a conversation with a union leader, who had told him that that the big threat and danger to our society would be an unknown virus sweeping the country. Which rather begs two questions, I feel. Firstly, why would the leader of the opposition give credibility on this subject to a trade union leader, rather than, say, an expert in virology and immunology, who he could quite easily chat to if he thought it important? And secondly, if you believed him, then why the **** did you not bother mentioning it until now, you complete tosser Corbyn!

26TH MARCH - LAUGH, I NEARLY BROKE THE VENTILATOR

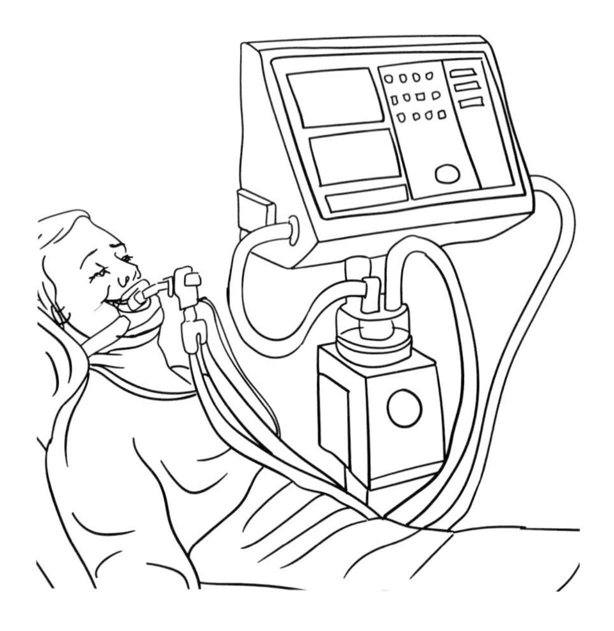

Normally, when disaster strikes, the jokes start almost immediately. The first recorded jokes about 9/11, for instance, were on 9/12. That's not a month later by the way, it's the day after. The Yanks haven't worked out how the bloody numbers work yet.

The first time people hear jokes about a disaster they often don't quite know how to react. They make a show of cringing or condemning - even if, inside, they actually think the joke is pretty funny. But after a while it becomes open season. Our inner reservations break down, and once they do, the boundary of bad taste gets pushed ever further. It's of the nature of tragedy for most of us that, unless we are in the inner circle of its impact, whilst we may associate with the tragedy when we first hear of it, its effect drains away quickly. If, for instance, we hear a news story of a coach crash in Turkey that has killed thirty school children, we are appalled and sad - particularly if we have kids of our own, so we can relate to it as parents. But not for long. Today's news is, as they say, tomorrow's chip paper. This doesn't make us awful people - the world is full of crises and tragedies, and humour is one important way we deal with this and normalise horror and pain. So, the further from the date of the event we get, the further away we are normally prepared to position the line of acceptable taste.

Consider this in the early days after the Grenfell Tower fire:

The Government has said there will be an amnesty on any illegal immigrants coming forward that were living in Grenfell towers, and they will be allowed to stay in the country for at least a year. So far thirty-one thousand people have come forward.

Funny, but more tangential to, rather than directly referencing, the horror of the event. You can probably imagine this one doing the rounds the day after the fire without too much backlash and indignation. Unless you happened to be an illegal, of course - but then again, probably not the smartest thing to make a deal of if you were. However, it too wasn't long before:

I was just about to raise my glass to the poor people that lost their lives in the recent London fire. Then I thought better not, they've already been toasted.

Which certainly more hardcore, even after time has wrought its healing effect, but enough water has passed under the bridge for it to now raise a smile. Well it did for me anyhow, but then I did make it up. If, however, we are directly related in some way to the tragedy, then it will never be funny. Not ever. I am guessing that the Bin Laden family think that jokes about him are never going to have them rolling in the isles. Though, personally, I think the idea of Osama having a DVD collection including:

Debby Does Abbottabad, Deep Goat, and Bare Ankles 4 is priceless. But, tell me a joke about Hillsborough, or even my brother's fetish for sniffing narcotics off Muslim wrestlers' jockstraps, and I'm likely to bristle. And even make a half-hearted attempt to deny the whole brother thing.

All of which brings me to the current crisis, and the state of coronavirus jokeage. There are plenty of funnies about - mostly memes, of course, as the world at large doesn't seem able to use the reading part of their brain in isolation any more - but it's all very tame so far. We are still at, to quote a phrase that has recently worked its way into the vernacular, the containment stage. Top of today's jokes list are such Tommy Cooper-like one-liners as:

Relief is … when two people come into the bank with masks - and tell us they're there for a hold-up.

Day Three without sports. Found a young lady sitting on my couch yesterday. Apparently, she's my wife. She seems nice.

Kid. 'Hey mum, when is this Coronavirus thing gonna be over'. Mum. 'Shut up son and eat your toilet paper.'

So, amusing, but no belly laughs, and certainly nothing to offend anyone as yet. But that will change in time I am sure. My guessing is that we will move through the phases of poor taste faster than Boris working his way through his different coronavirus strategies. We will definitely be getting very close to the knuckle at some stage soon. But, for those of you in hospital worst affected by the virus, some words of hope from Vera Lynn, the nation's sweetheart during our last great national emergency, 'We'll breathe again, don't know where, don't know when ….'

27TH MARCH - CELEBRITIES - HOW LUCKY WE ARE TO HAVE THEM!

I've never had much truck with celebrities. Mainly because I'm not one, of course, but also because the average celeb's conceptualisation of himself or herself is quite irritatingly ridiculous. Not only do celebs have fame and fortune, they appear to feel immensely entitled to it, no matter how mediocre their talent or personality. As Descartes would almost certainly comment, if he were around to update his landmark work, *The Meditations*, with a more modern slant: 'I preen, therefore I am.' Given this, one might think this whole self-isolation thing should bring the worst out of them; we might expect them to pontificate as though it was they who were the centre of attention in this whole thing, that the real reason the world is going to pot is that we just aren't seeing enough of them strutting their stuff. Well, I couldn't have been more wrong! Thank heaven for social media, that's all I can say. Through its various incarnations, we are able to access the celeb in his/her isolation, and we are fortunate indeed to have our celebs here to help us through these troubled times.

Take Madonna, for instance. 'That's the thing about Covid-19. It doesn't care about how rich you are, how famous you are, how funny you are, how smart you are, where you live, how old you are, or what amazing stories you can tell. It's the great equaliser and what's terrible about it is what's great about it.' Madonna enlightened us with this insight whilst filming herself naked in a milky bath full of rose petals. As you do. That single mother on the seventh floor of a tower block in Lambeth must be releived to know that, despite the fact she increasingly wants to throw her kids off the balcony, all other things between her and Madge are now equal!

Someone called Cardi B, who is a hip-hop singer apparently (which means she can't actually sing at all, I imagine) and who allegedly has more than sixty million followers, stood up for all her fellow Americans over the weekend with a right good anti-establishment rant about what she felt was a lack of information and action from the US government. 'When they put Wuhan, China, in quarantine… they were spraying [stuff] in the streets. They were knocking on each door taking people's temperature. Let's say that I have the coronavirus right now, OK? How am I supposed to know I got it?' Now Cardi might admittedly be overlooking a minor point - that the reason the Chinese had to take such action was because they were so criminally negligent when the virus first emerged - but, nevertheless, she has emerged as the true spokesman for the common person in the street, artistically standing up to the 'Man' like a latter day Bob Dylan. I think the lyrics from one of her songs, *Weave*, capture what we're all thinking really:

The nerve of you bitches
Like, oh my God, I got no words for you bitches
Like, who's really serving you bitches? need some answers, I'm worried for bitches
Like, this really absurd
No wonder these niggas stay curving you bitches
Don't even take no more selfies
That weave don't even deserve any pictures

The other great thing about celebrities is how keen they are to selflessly promote the right social messages. Take Kevin Bacon, for instance. Now, you might have thought he was just that annoying tosser who does the EE adverts, but no, this is a man who is truly doing his bit. 'Hey everybody, it's now so important to stay home and keep our distance from others if you are able. It's one way we can help prevent the spread of #Coronavirus and save lives. The more of us who can make it safer for those who can't. So, if you're home too like me, post a video or photo with a sign like mine, telling who you are staying home for and ask 6 friends to do the same. Post it with the hashtag #IStayHomeFor so I can see and share. The more folks involved, the merrier - We're all connected by various degrees (Trust me, I know!) I'm kicking it off with @jimmyfallon @eltonjohn @Brandicarlile @kevinhart4real @ddlovato @davidbeckham - but I encourage YOU ALL to join in too! Let's use this 6 Degree thing to do some good.'

Now, some unkind people might say that Kevin really only wanted to show us how many famous friends he has (and to pop in a little promo for his advertising cash-cow with the 'we're all connected' reference). Well, hang your heads in shame, you cynics. Kevin's initiative may save lives, and I for one think he should be applauded. And ideally given such a large amount of money he never needs to work - or ideally be seen - on TV again!

But when it comes to mates, Kevin is the lonely kid on the block compared to Gal Gadot, the Wonder Woman actress, who shared a video of herself and all her chums singing individual lines of Imagine to cheer us up. To accompany this she posted, 'We are in this together, we will get through it together. Let's imagine together. Sing with us ❤ All love to you, from me and my dear friends. #WeAreOne .... #KristenWiig #JamieDornan @labrinth @james_marsden @sarahkatesilverman @eddiebenjamin @jimmyfallon @natalieportman @zoeisabellakravitz @siamusic @reallyndacarter @amyadams @leslieodomjr @pascalispunk @chrisodowd @hotpatooties #WillFerrell @markruffalo @norahjones @ashleybenson @kaiagerber @caradelevingne @anniemumolo @princesstagramslam.'

It may be an absolutely cringe-makingly awful rendition - and, unlike the sentiment in the song, I am struggling to imagine any of this crew without rather a lot of possessions if I'm completely honest - but let's not ruin such a special moment with such trivia. The main thing is that we've seen lots and lots of caring celebs, all showing that they are the kind of role models who can cope with the world going to pot - with good cheer, and a lovely singalong. And how uplifting is that?

Bored with being stuck at home? No worries. There is no shortage of celebs generous enough to show you how to while away a happy hour or so. Jake Quickenden sent out a video of himself pretending to play quidditch, while hovering in mid-air on a makeshift broomstick on his couch. It's mildly possible I might get a tad bit annoyed if any of my boys did this - they're not fifteen yet, and Jake is thirty-one, for fuck's sake. But, hey, Jake has been on the X-factor twice, and I'm a Celebrity too, so I guess I'm happy he's leading the way and showing us that's the kind of wacky stuff we could be doing, if only we have the imagination and zest for life of the Celeb. As well as flying about on his Nimbus 2000, Jake challenged *Dancing on Ice* star Perri Keily to the teabag challenge. I thought this was going to be a bit more like it, if I'm honest, though I wasn't sure how he would square tea-bagging with social distancing. But it basically just involved throwing your teabag into the mug with one attempt. Which was something of a let-down really. I'm not sure it will make it into the Olympics, but as the Celebs are doing it, who knows? I, for one, would welcome it with open arms. Perhaps replacing the hundred metres?

But of course, no essay on celebrities would be complete without a mention of those Celebrities-in-Chief, the Beckhams. David and Victoria have been generously taking the time to stream videos of themselves baking on their Instragram channel. It's a bit off the wall, these two getting into the food porn game, as Victoria clearly doesn't eat a whole lot, and David looks like he is sustained entirely by ink injections. But anyways, in their most recent video, Victoria was talking her twenty-eight million Instagram followers through the recipe when a rude noise could be heard in the background. 'That's the dog! That was the dog making that noise.' Victoria laughs.

'Don't lie.' David quickly hits back. 'Seriously, we know you had baked beans for lunch.'

Top banter indeed!

I take it all back, they're all tw**s. The bloody lot of them.

28TH MARCH - TOMORROW WILL BE DIFFERENT

Over the last few days, I have heard many people telling us that this is a seminal moment, that nothing will be the same after we get through the worst of this crisis. That, somehow, this would have taught humanity a lesson, that this is the Universe's way of telling us we need to get back to basic decency. There is much made of the sterling work of our hospital staff; of the fantastic response of the many good people who have volunteered to help in their communities over the last few days. The narrative (even though, as you know, I hate that word) is of a world that is kinder, more caring, less transfixed with materialism. A world chastened, and ready to learn from the lessons it is being dealt. If this were true, I would be thrilled. But, and I don't want to be a party pooper here, I'm afraid I don't buy it at all. I wish I did, but I don't. Sadly, I think we will come out of this unchanged: both as people individually, and as humanity collectively. The good lessons we hope will have embedded themselves in our collective psyche, like so much virus into our archetypal cells, will be overwhelmed by the antibodies within our societal structure which fight against them. Put simply, the nature of the people who tend to gravitate to power, and the very structure of the economics that govern our world, will overpower any good intentions of the masses.

Now, I don't wish to sound this pessimistic, but I am. I have believed that, when the answers to the questions you ask are not delivering the solutions you want, you are probably asking the wrong questions. I am also inclined to the view that the right questions are normally simple; they are not complicated or complex. I suspect this is a perspective I share with Albert Einstein. Not that I am not seeking comparisons with the great man (unless you want to make them of course), since I manifestly don't have his genius. (Though my hair is way better than his, and in the great scheme of things I would like to think this makes for an honourable draw. Though I'm relatively certain Albert would have bloody killed for my hair, so he may have me edging the whole thing.) Anyhow, I digress. Let me get back to trying to ask the questions which will hopefully provide a platform to try to explain why I think nothing will change.

My first question is this.

Are individual people able to drive collective change?

Vilfredo Pareto, in *Cours d'économie* politique, showed that approximately eighty per cent of the land in Italy was owned by twenty per cent of the population. This became known as the eighty/twenty law, and, astonishingly, this eighty/twenty ratio seems able to be successfully applied to almost any endeavour in life. As examples: eighty per cent of your results will probably come from twenty per cent of your effort, and eighty per cent of a company's income will come from twenty per cent of its customers. It's amazing how applicable the concept is. I have my own premise: eighty per cent of people are decent, caring and nice people; twenty per cent are not. I suspect you are with me so far - most people are good people, and 80/20 probably isn't an unreasonable division. But let's consider the twenty per cent who are not decent, and drill further down, again using the eighty/twenty rule. Of this group, let's assume that eighty per cent are just hopeless, lazy wasters. General low-life, for want of a better description. This leaves twenty per cent of this group who are different in some way - or four per cent of the total population. Now, coincidentally, psychologists are of the view that four per cent of the population are sociopaths - which is interesting - mainly because it makes my own maths work perfectly. And, of the four per cent of people who are sociopaths, amazingly, the eighty/twenty rule works again- around twenty per cent are psychopaths.

But what is a sociopath, and how does he/she differ from a psychopath? Well, Psychopaths and sociopaths share a number of characteristics, including: a lack of remorse or empathy for others, a lack of guilt, an inability to take responsibility for their actions, a disregard for laws or social conventions, and an inclination to violence. Core, to both a psychopath and a sociopath, is a deceitful and manipulative nature. But how can we tell them apart? Well, apparently, sociopaths are normally less emotionally stable and highly impulsive - their behaviour tends to be more erratic than psychopaths. When committing crimes - either violent or non-violent - sociopaths will act more on compulsion; they will lack patience, giving in much more easily to impulsiveness and lacking detailed planning. Psychopaths, on the other hand, will plan their crimes down to the smallest detail, taking calculated risks to avoid detection. The smart ones will leave few clues that may lead to being caught. Psychopaths don't get carried away in the moment and make fewer mistakes as a result. Here is a list of the professions that are believed are most attractive to the psychopath - it is quite startling (this ranking is compiled by Oxford psychologist Kevin Dutton, author of The Wisdom of Psychopaths: What Saints, Spies, and Serial Killers Can Teach Us About Success):

1. CEO
2. Lawyer
3. Media (TV/Radio)
4. Salesperson
5. Surgeon
6. Journalist
7. Police Officer
8. Clergy Person
9. Chef
10. Civil Servant

So, if we add to this the fact most senior politicians come from a background in business or law, an astonishingly high proportion of our leaders, right across society, have core characteristics which include a lack of remorse or empathy for others, and a lack of guilt or ability to take responsibility for their actions. To put it bluntly, an astonishing proportion of the people with real power probably aren't reacting to the situation today in the same way as the eighty per cent of us who see ourselves as good and decent people. Donald Trump, and a number of senior American politicians, for example, very clearly see the situation today far less in terms of human tragedy than in hardnosed economic terms. Whilst we, as a majority, may want to learn the lessons we are being taught, those same lessons will wash over the psychopathic minority who are psychologically programmed in a completely different way.

And, if this wasn't bad enough, we are structured economically in such a way that we are incapable of reacting positively, even if we so wished. Communism failed; spectacularly so. Like all Utopian ideals, it took little account of the selfish motivations of the individual, nor of the fact that the people who rise to the top are very likely to be psychopaths rather than idealists, so communist regimes inevitably came to be run by complete bastards. In the end, capitalism has triumphed - largely because it plays very well to the desire most of us have to better ourselves. This is an positive thing, of course it is, but unchecked it stokes an unsustainable flame. And that flame is continued growth in GDP, and this is the flame in which all our hopes for a better world look set to be consumed.

So, my second question: Can our obsession with GDP be changed?

There are few of us who don't feel happy when we hear the economy is growing, and panicked when we hear words like 'recession'. But if we took the time to think about it, we all know continual growth is unsustainable. If we grow by just two per cent per annum for the next hundred years, this means that GDP will need to be more than seven times greater than it is today. And no matter how many 'soft services' this involves, this basically means that we will have to produce a ridiculous amount more crap in a hundred years' time than we do today. This, at a time when the little matter of climate change is threatening to wipe us out if we continue on the path we are treading. But, since the corollary to growth would appear to be recession - and since no-one wants to lose their house or their job - growth is the hamster wheel on which humanity today pedals faster and faster.

So, where are we? What is the big picture? Well, I think it is this. We inhabit a world that conducts itself based on an impossible growth strategy, run by people who, frankly, don't give a shit, and don't look at life like the rest of us. Against this backdrop, do you really see a changed world when we come out of this? I've told you my view. I hope the optimists amongst us are right, and I am wrong. I really do.

POSTSCRIPT

After writing this I went onto my iPhone, and saw a HuffPost article, part of which I copy below. I rest my case!

'The White House chose the week the United States became the epicentre of a historic pandemic to virtually stop policing big polluters, privatize a bedrock federal food safety job, advance a mining road through a pristine swath of northern Alaska and revive a regulatory rollback so difficult to defend that the Trump administration abandoned the effort last year at the peak of a high-profile fight.

On Thursday afternoon, the Environmental Protection Agency announced it would suspend enforcement of bedrock clean air and water laws, leaving the fossil fuel, chemical and agribusiness industries to police themselves amid a historic public health crisis.

Hours later, the U.S. Department of Agriculture confirmed a waiver allowing a private company to take over inspection duties at a Tyson Foods beef slaughterhouse.

By Friday morning, news broke that the administration was close to finalizing its plan to roll back Obama-era rules raising fuel-economy standards on new vehicles, resuming a fight that delighted the oil industry, divided automakers and revealed a double standard on states' rights as the White House sought to bring California to its knees. And by midday, the administration published a final review of a proposed 211-mile road that would cut through a portion of Alaska's Gates of the Arctic National Park and Preserve and open up an area rich in copper, zinc and other minerals.'

29TH MARCH - THE GOOD, THE BAD AND THE UGLY

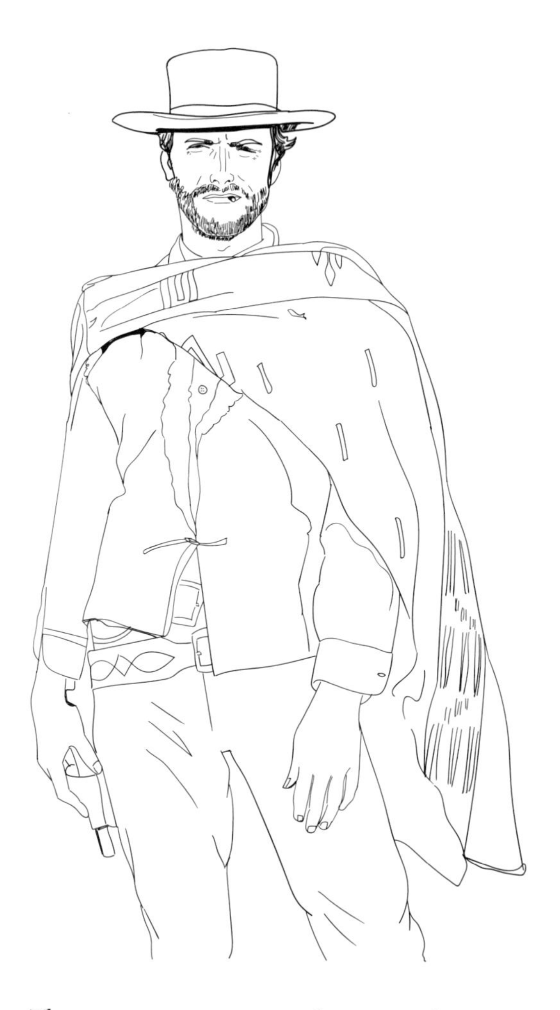

There was an expression that came about in World War Two to describe someone's activity a conflict. 'He had a good war.' they would say. Unquestionably, this was seen as a good thing. Apart from anything else it meant that you were still alive, and that you'd probably avoided having your leg shot off, or your testicles mashed into an unidentifiable compote. Which was definitely a bonus. It probably meant too that, either you were lucky enough to have been 'in action' at some hot spots where your side had done well, or that you had been there during some unmitigated and awe-inspiring catastrophe from which survival itself was deemed heroic. The long and short of it: you had either done something stupidly brave, or you'd just been in the wrong place at the right time and lived to tell the tale. That was a good war. You survived. Bits intact. Then, if you'd had a good war, someone in power (who had almost certainly been a long way away from the action) pinned a ribbon with a dangly bit of metal onto your chest. And, when you were down the pub back at home, you had a sporting chance of parleying that medal into a quick shag with an impressionable bit of nonsense at the Cock and Foreplay, while you tried not to have flashbacks about your mate screaming and trying to keep his spleen in his stomach, or wondering how you'll cope on the dole now that you've missed out on your youth and your education.

But times have moved on. Our enemy today doesn't have human form - much though The Donald would love to give it slanty eyes and a takeaway menu - but all the talk is of a war, nonetheless. We are, quite literally, bunkering in against the blitz. The enemy is out there. We can't hear him; can't see him. But we can be sure he is there. Lurking on every door handle; hovering like tiny, unseen Vietcong in the mucal aftermath of every sneeze and cough. A cruel sniper of the shadows, picking off the old and the underlyingly-unhealthy. We are all in the vanguard of this new war. So, who is having a good war so far, and who is not? Who are the Good, the Bad and the Ugly of this war?

THE GOOD

Well, you can't travel far on this track without saying 'NHS', clearly. To say otherwise would be tantamount to treason in these troubled times, so, even if I had a mind to (which I don't) I would be insane to say anything but good things about our health service and the many fantastic people in it. If Italy is anything to go by, things will get worse, and quite literally our doctors and nurses will be working in field conditions. A thought too, though, for the much-maligned administrators of the NHS. I have worked delivering services to the NHS for the better part of thirty years, and a thorn in my side - and many like me - is the sluggishness and the turgidity of decision making. Not now. Big decisions are being made with alacrity. The torpor of the NHS has been thrown off, and I, for one, hope this new rugged-jaw approach will become the norm when the dark night gives way to a more promising dawn.

But it's not just the NHS; it is us as a community at large. We have responded to the new enemy with humour, determination and grit. Half a million people have volunteered to help in twenty-four hours. No pay. No reward. Just people who want to do the right thing for other people. Individual support groups have sprung up faster than daffodils on a warm day in March. Sections of our community normally hardly noticed - supermarket workers for instance - have become the new heroes. They are having a good war.

And in fairness, despite a less than commendable amount of early dithering, Boris is having a pretty good war too. Though he is lucky to have the rat-like Jeremy Corbyn in the other corner: Chamberlain to his Churchill. But we have, at last, seen the decisiveness we crave from a leader, and we are behind him. And he's taken a bullet too. The enemy has breached his inner sanctum, and Boris now leads from the isolation of his ventilated bunker - with the halo of the saviour wrapping him in the affection of the nation. It's made him one of us, he has the scar on his cheek of the true warrior - and we all love the fact that we absolutely know this is definitely a man who will parley that into a bonk down at the Swan and Semen when this isolation ends. Get in there my old son.

And one final contender for the 'good' category? You'll find this hard to believe, but Simon Cowell. Diminutive egotistical tosser that he is, Simon has donated a million dollars towards the immediate needs of some of the most vulnerable people impacted by this virus. He also issued a clarion call to other celebrities bunkered down in their fabulous mansions. 'I don't like celebrities telling people what to do, and I know this is a hugely difficult time for so many - worries about family, health, jobs, paying the mortgage and feeding their family are at the forefront of people's minds. But there are still other people in business and in entertainment with resources available. So today it's those people I'm urging to rise to this enormous challenge. The wealthy donors and corporate organisations I'm talking about. I hope that if any good can come from this awful crisis it might be that people everywhere start to see the world a little differently.' Good on you Simon. Not quite a Golden Buzzer, but you are definitely through to Boot Camp mate.

THE BAD

Wars, as they say, bring out the worst in people. Nothing provides the opportunity to get rich faster than a war. The economics of war present a myriad of opportunities to the unscrupulous and the unprincipled. There was hardly a German company of any standing, for instance, which didn't take advantage of the opportunities given to them by the Nazis. I G Farben (which in 1951 split into Bayer, BASF and Hoerst) actually built the concentration camp at Auschwitz and was its legal owner. It was Farben that developed and sold the poison gas - Zyklon B - used in the gas chambers. Siemens operated one of the Auschwitz subcamps. Ferdinand Porsche, then working for Volkswagen, contacted SS leader Heinrich Himmler directly to request for slaves from Auschwitz. Wars reward bad people, and there is never a shortage of bad people coming out of the shadows in search of those rewards. So, who are the bad people in this war?

Well, some of them are us. The people who think it is macho not to isolate, quite content that the consequence of their actions might be the unnecessary death of someone's loved parent or grandparent. The people who, even though they very clearly only have one arse, think it is OK to buy enough toilet paper to accommodate all the enormous arses down at Old Trafford put together. The shopkeepers who put up prices for everyday commodities, just because they can, oblivious to the old and the vulnerable who simply can't afford to pay. And, of course, where there is big business, there will always be the sociopaths and psychopaths who make it to the top. I'm no Trump fan, and you would be an idiot to believe a word that comes out of his mouth, but his tiff with GE this week does have a ring of truth about it. Trump tweeted. 'They said they were going to give us forty thousand much needed Ventilators, 'very quickly'. Now they are saying it will only be 6000, in late April, and they want top dollar'. It really would be nice to think that GE, a company with total assets in excess of $300,000,000,000 (that's three hundred billion!), might actually put helping people who are dying above thrashing out the most profitable deal for itself. Just once.

And big Pharma, as ever, is on the naughty step. The pharmaceutical industry worldwide generates worldwide revenues of over $1TN (I've never written one trillion dollars before - I think that's how it's done). Half of this revenue comes into US companies, and across the sector it delivers twenty-one per cent margin. It is, by a measure, the most profitable of any major industry. Back to Trump, though. I was pretty sceptical about his claim that hydroxychloroquine, a drug used in the treatment of malaria, might be the answer to a maiden's prayer in the quest for an inoculation against coronavirus. His claim had the ring of the desperate looking for a miracle. And, of course, it might not work. But no trials whatsoever have commenced in the US to test his claim. Most of the big pharma companies, however, have commenced trials on their own pet solutions. The reason they have ignored hydroxychloroquine?

It's not proprietary to one company, so there are no big bucks to be gained by pushing it. On the basis Trump started the dialogue, I wouldn't have necessarily popped the Pharma industry in the 'bad' category if I hadn't spotted an article about a French trial this week. I quote: 'On Tuesday, a team of French scientists released the first results of a clinical study of the use of hydroxychloroquine on 24 coronavirus patients from southeast France. The research team, led by Didier Raoult, a renowned infectious disease expert from l'Institut Hospitalo-Universitaire in Marseille, administered the drug for ten days along with azithromycin, a common antibiotic. Researchers said the drugs cleared the virus in the nose and throat of most observed patients in three to six days. The study found that after six days of treatment, seventy per cent of patients administered hydroxychloroquine were clear of the virus, compared to just twleve and a half per cent percent of patients who were not given drugs. Azithromycin boosted the effect of hydroxychloroquine, according to the study. After six days of treatment, all patients treated with the drug combination "were virologically cured," compared to fifty-seven point one percent of patients treated with hydroxycholorquine by itself.' In other words, it might just bloody work! But an industry, purportedly dedicated to solving our healthcare problems, would much rather it didn't. There is definitely a special part of hell reserved for those boys.

THE UGLY

Mention the word 'ugly' and my mind immediately goes to two things.: politicians and Diane Abbott. Well I guess that's only one thing if you want to be pedantic, as Diane is both. But I am sure you will be grateful that I'm not going to focus on Ms. Abbott in particular - though, in fairness, she might prove a godsent in helping us balance the books after all of this, given her much quoted statement during an LBS interview that, 'If we recruit ten thousand police men and women over a four-year period, we believe it'll cost about three hundred thousand pounds.'

But I'm talking 'ugly' about politicians in general. Now, clearly, Trump leads the way in the ugliness stakes by almost the same distance as Liverpool lead the Premier League, but at least he has the virtue of being completely transparent. There is no other side to The Donald. Other politicians, however, hide beneath a veneer of makeup to cover up their innate ugliness. Take this from Emmanuel Macron: 'France is alongside Italy.' he told us in an interview with Italian newspapers La Repubblica and La Stampa, a day after Italy logged its worst one-day death toll yet - recording 969 new deaths. 'There is a lot of talk about Chinese or Russian aid, but why don't we say that France and Germany have delivered two million masks, and tens of thousands gowns, to Italy? What worries me is the illness of every man for himself: if we do not show solidarity, Italy, Spain or others would be able to say to their European partners: where have you been when we were at the front? I do not want this selfish and divided Europe.' Too little, too late, Emmanuel. Both France and Germany initially declined to provide Rome with face masks and other equipment to help it handle their outbreak. The great proponents of 'One Europe wanted to keep all of their goodies to themselves. As my Dad used to say, you can never trust the frogs or the krauts in a war. Rome turned for help to China instead, which sent an airplane full of masks and ventilators, bearing 'Forza Italia' stickers with small Chinese and Italian flags, and leaving a powerful and lasting impression on the Italians.

This brings me to the Chinese. Having created this human catastrophe with their (allegedly) appalling negligence, they took the right steps eventually to get themselves out of the crap. They could have let things settle at that, of course. And it seems harsh to talk badly of them when they are shipping out their people and supplies to help stricken countries like Italy. But there is a big bit of me that thinks that the Chinese rulers are far less concerned about the humanitarian crisis they have precipitated, than about dropping the Chinese flag on territories where it craves influence. Call me an old cynic.

So, there we have it. The Good, the Bad and the Ugly. Feel free to make comments with your own nominations, and have a great isolated Sunday.

30TH MARCH - AND THE AWARD FOR STAYING INDOORS GOES TO ...

We are repeatedly being beseeched to stay indoors. Often by the Prime Minister, who earlier this month was out and about happily shaking hands with patients in a hospital in Kettering. No good was ever going to come of that: Boris now has the virus, and the patients' families won't talk to them anymore. But most often we are being told it by Piers Morgan, who has clearly voted himself spokesman-in-chief for telling us all what to do. Regrettably, I quite often find myself agreeing with Piers, but that doesn't mean he's not a complete dick. Or, 'bell-end', as Vinnie

Jones called him today in his birthday card for Piers', that Piers read out just to prove how popular he is amongst the glitterati. This was just before he told us what a wonderful idea his great friend Cheryl Tweedy/Cole/Fernadez-Versini had about food shopping. Tweeted Cheryl:

I have an idea. I haven't got into any of the logistics yet but as a concept ..as there are now so many drive through restaurants closed.. could we partner them with food stores, set up an app for locals and use their drive thru's as a safer way for ppl to shop essentials?

Replying to a fan, she also added:

So, there would be an app and I guess like click and collect. But you would order and then collect it through the window at the drive thru. But for essentials.

I love how Cheryl tells us that she, 'Hasn't got into any of the logistics yet'. I can imagine her at home, as we speak, working out loadings and routing maps, talking to DHL about how this will all work, and at the same time knocking out a bit of coding for her app to interface with Waitrose's stock system. And here's me thinking she was just a self-promoting, really mediocre singer with an indecipherable accent. Wow - how wrong could I be! Anyhow, since Piers has the hots for Cheryl, he opined that this was a jolly good idea. It's not Piers. I'm not sure whether you've ever been to a McDonald's drive-through, but the window you get served your Big Mac from might be ok for passing over small bags of very light food, but it would be bloody hopeless for handing over big bags of heavy shopping filled with essentials. Like beer and wine and large bars of chocolate. They also normally have small car parks, so all this would create is queues and chaos. Supermarkets, on the other, have very big car parks. They also have the great benefit of the food being there in the first place. So, it surely makes much more sense to use this as a starting point if we don't want people in the actual shops. Just a thought.

But I've gone off on a bit of a tangent with Cheryl. The point I really wanted to make was that I can't quite understand why Piers himself is not staying indoors. When did *Good Morning Britain* become an essential service? And, in any event, why could he not deliver his sermons from his home, rather than commuting to and from Television Centre every day? We certainly have the technology - as the rest of us know only too well in this working-from-home-world we now inhabit. But Piers must be doing something right, as odds of him becoming Prime Minister by 2040 have incredibly been slashed - from five hundred to one, to fifty to one. It might actually be fun if he was PM (though I do remember thinking the same thing about Trump). At Prime Minister's Question time, for instance, we could install a panel in front of the Dispatch Box, with the Leader of the Opposition, the Speaker of the House and Cheryl Tweedy/Cole/Ferndadez-Versini - all commenting and voting on the quality of Piers' answers to MPs questions. 'Yee owned that despatch box pet, well dyun. But ah think yee need to explain betta how HS2 will benefit the fowk of the Toon. And why it cannae stop at MacDonald's. It's a ne frem me.' It would be compulsive viewing. Better than *Good Morning Britain*, that's for sure.

But Piers doesn't even make the top two on the leader board when it comes to the award for worst going-outside-for non-essential business offender. In second place we have Stephen Kinnock, the MP for Aberavon. Stephen, and his wife, drove over one hundred and fifty miles to see his dad on his birthday. He then was stupid enough to tell us all about this on Twitter:

Dad turned 78 today. Incredible, but true. Helle Thorning-Schmidt and I took a couple of chairs over, and sat in their front garden for a socially distanced celebration. As you do Happy birthday, mate.

Apart from the inherent oddness of referring to his wife by her full name, this is, after all, an MP. I know he's a Labour MP, and this probably makes him a bit dim, but what is it he doesn't understand about staying inside and not buggering off on long journeys? According to the Daily Mail, the Police, 'blasted' Stephen for his reckless behaviour. What they actually did was tweet to him, and say:

Hello Stephen Kinnock, we know celebrating your Dad's birthday is a lovely thing to do, however this is not essential travel. We all have our part to play in this, we urge you to comply with government restrictions, they are in place to keep us all safe. Thank you.

Phew, I hope the South Wales Police never blast me. Brutal! The police in Mumbai, who are beating people with sticks when they are caught outside, have got nothing on these boys. Anyhow, Stephen replied an hour later:

I felt that this was essential travel as I had to deliver some necessary supplies to my parents. I stayed long enough to sing 'Happy Birthday' to Dad, and then I was off. All the best, Stephen.

Well, that tweet may only be two lines long, but, right off the bounce, there are two clear porkies here. First off, his dad is that old windsock Neil Kinnock. For those of you who remember Neil, he never once in his life uttered a sentence that took less than an hour to complete. So, no way you were in and out with just a 'Happy Birthday', Stevie-boy. And secondly, my recollection is that the Kinnocks live in Ealing, where, to the best of my knowledge they have rather a lot of shops. It is hard to know what essential supplies Stevie might be able to find in Aberavon which aren't available in Ealing. Particularly to people with the influence of Neil and Glenys. So, Stephen clearly gave an appalling example to the rest of us, that ill-befits his role as an MP, and which, I am guessing, doesn't make it any easier for the police to enforce isolation on ordinary people who would rather like to spend time with loved ones on special occasions. Still, at least it runs in the family. Steven's sister, Rachel tweeted that she had popped over to Mum and Dad's to deliver a cake, a crumble and a lovely lamb curry. Ah, that's nice!

You would think this might make Steven the winner of *Worst Offender* award hands down, but amazingly, he has been pipped at the post. Not because the winning offence was worse, just much funnier. Mind you, pretty well anything is funnier that the Kinnocks. My winner of the day is the driver who drove down from Coventry to Salford to pick up some windows he had bought for fifteen pounds on eBay. When he was stopped by a police check on the M6 in Cheshire on Sunday, after collecting his purchase, the police found his wife in the boot. Apparently, she couldn't fit in the car once the windows had been loaded up. Now that's what I call top social distancing!

31ST MARCH - THERE'S PLENTY TO DO….

Well, it's two weeks since we drew up the drawbridge, and I'm struggling to understand why people might be getting even a tiny bit bored. But, for those of you who are, here are my Top Ten Tips of how best to while away the self-isolated hours.

1. Grow a beard. I am only a couple of days in but this is already giving me countless hours of pleasure, as I endlessly stroke my emerging whiskers. My wife, for some odd reason, seems to think it is a terrible idea, and calls me things like 'vagrant' and 'scruffbag'. Well I've been called much worse, so that's not going get me searching for the razor. So, she threatened divorce. Not that's she's the type to go nuclear at the mildest provocation, you understand. But I cunningly pointed out that she can't leave at the moment, as we're confined to barracks. So she informed me that all kissing would stop until I had a shave. It didn't seem to go down too well when I asked her whether this was just her, or whether this was a blanket ban? God, she's touchy. And now, she's resorted to blackmail. I have to buy her something every day that I continue the hirsute madness. So, tomorrow, her new hoover comes, and on Thursday the paint for the bedroom arrives. Frankly, she should have just kept quiet - I wasn't actually growing a beard at all, I just got a bit lazy during lockdown.

2. Encourage your children to read. Now a word of warning here, only attempt this if you really want to hear your kids bleating and moaning like you'd asked them to pop up the chimney and give it a good clean. When I was their age, I hated broccoli. Well, it appears that books are new broccoli. My boys bloody hate them, and think they serve no purpose whatsoever. Asking them to read is like a punishment. Drop your trousers boy, and read six of the best! Actually, maybe I should delete that sentence - it doesn't sound quite right for some reason. Oh, sod it! At least the boys will never bloody read it. Though, funny enough, the only thing I've persuaded them to read is the first few pages of the book I wrote. (I just thought I'd drop that in again: you can download it onto your kindle, or order a beautiful hardback coffee table version from Amazon. It makes a wonderful Xmas, Birthday or Lockdown

present). Even my boys couldn't think of an excuse not to read their Dad's book - even if they do think it's shit.

3. Play Monopoly. For a full three hours of shouting, bitching, cheating and general unpleasantness, you can't beat it. We have the Liverpool FC version, where the familiar London landmarks are replaced by Liverpool players and managers. I hate the game anyway, but it is truly torture when every time you throw the dice you land on 'Home' (Community Chest, in real money), or 'Away' (Chance), so you can't actually buy anything. I wish I'd bought the Manchester United version; no-one would want to buy those fuckers anyway. The Liverpool version of the game did, however, manage to both combine political correctness and misogyny rather brilliantly. It had a number of women from Liverpool Ladies team, but quite rightly made sure that these were only the really cheap properties, the ones right after you pass 'go'. There were definitely no girls anywhere near Piccadilly. Well, not unless you played your 'Away' card, and ordered one up on-line. It was also strangely anti-Belgian. Divock Origi didn't manage to make the cut at all for some strange reason - which was pretty amazing when you consider Nathaniel Clyne was in the Pall Mall position, and Simon Mignolet in the Old Kent Road spot with the girls. I hear he pulled one of the girls, by the way, but, true to form, dropped her very quickly.

4. Go for a walk with the kids. What could be more delightful on a nice afternoon! If one of them decides to be in a sulk for no apparent reason and walk about a quarter of a mile ahead, that really adds to the whole family-fun thing. And if you can persuade your youngest to put on his best whiney voice, and gripe the entire time about how he wants a hedgehog in his bedroom, then all the better. No wonder Boris only lets us have one walk a day!

5. Sit in a quiet room, with an ice-pack on your head and you best thinking cap set squarely to 'action', and try to work out what on earth you should be doing to make sure your business is in decent shape when this madness ends. Nah ... that one's best put off till tomorrow I reckon.

6. Apply for the next series of Mastermind. I already have my specialist subjects sorted and in good shape, but over the coming days and weeks I get sharper than a sharpie thing, and will have them off pat by the time I'm sitting in the black chair chatting with Magnus. Round 1: Frasier. Semi-final: Peaky Blinders. Final: Coronavirus statistics between March 21 and March 29th.

7. Get your kids to write a journal. On second thoughts, don't. It gets to be a teensy bit repetitive. Got up. Had breakfast. Played Minecraft. Had lunch. Played football. Argued about reading with Dad. Played football. Had dinner. Played FIFA. Repeat.

8. Cook. Or at least I think it's called cooking. I'm pretty sure that's what it's called when you wander into the kitchen, and someone gives you a cup of tea and some boiled eggs. Then tells you to sod off, while she buggers off and runs a half marathon, before picking some nettles to make nettle soup for lunch. Before murdering a very surprised chicken. to put the coq into the coq au van for the evening. Or is that just my house? Whatever, it's bloody hard work being on the receiving end of all that I can tell you.

9. Do some gardening. If you want to really push the boat out, invite your children to help you in the garden. This will involve a two-hour argument so draining you never actually make it out into the garden. It's brilliant: no matter how long this lockdown goes on, I

will still be happy in the knowledge that there is plenty to do out there to keep me from going bonkers.

10. DIY. The best way to do this, I am reliably told, is to buy some gear on eBay. Preferably located as far away as possible. Then go and pick this up in a very small car, whilst working out how to avoid police roadblocks and making sure that your wife is nice and comfy in the boot - with a good cookbook and the Monopoly.

Happy days!

1ST APRIL - WHO'S THE FOOL NOW?

Am I the only person who half expected to wake up this morning with a message from Boris telling us this has all been an elaborate April Fool's Joke? That we should all have a good chuckle and head back off to work? Trump is doing something similar in America - albeit in a reverse psychology kind of way. Only a few days after telling Americans that large parts of the country would be, 'Open for business by 12th April.' and almost a month to the day since he told us that, 'It's going to disappear. One day - it's like a miracle - it will disappear.' his latest update warned Americans to be prepared for the hard days that lie ahead. 'We're going to go through a tough two weeks.' he said, projecting a death toll of a hundred thousand or more. Though this didn't stop him for claiming that the measures he has taken have prevented a death toll in the US that could have hit two point two million. I can only imagine how well this sort of line in in self-congratulation would be received were it to be proffered by a company director in court defending a criminal negligence prosecution. 'Your honour, I know five people died falling through the hole in the floor that I didn't bother to fix for three weeks. But, let's look on the good side. I put some boarding there after a while - it probably saved the life of the other hundred people I employ. You should be thanking me really.' A favourite little ditty from the Trump campaign in 2016, referring to Hilary Clinton, was that they should, 'Lock her up'. Was ever anything more ironic?

But Trump is not alone across the world. There are many countries whose sociopath leaders have tried to put a band aid on a wound that is spurting blood. An estimated three hundred and fifty thousand displaced people across Myanmar are sitting in the path of a public health catastrophe. Overcrowding, movement restrictions and poor sanitation have left these groups especially vulnerable to the coronavirus outbreak. Myanmar had its first infections last week. and its first death on Monday. A government official had previously claimed that the country's lifestyle and diet protected its people. Belarus' President Alexander Lukashenko has shrugged off concerns about Covid-19, telling his people that hockey, vodka, and a sauna are the best cures. Ostriches, burying their head in the sand, would be funny where the repercussions are not so awful.

April Fool's Day, however, should be funny. Though not if you are to believe Nate Scott, a journalist writing on the USA Today website. 'If you think an April Fool's joke would be funny today, you are wrong. This is not the time. Every year come April Fool's Day, some brand and/or practical joker with limited imagination thinks it'll be fun to pull an April Fool's joke. First off: April Fool's jokes aren't jokes. There is never a set up nor a payoff. They usually involve lying to people, and then making them feel stupid. They are not jokes, they are lies. Which, means they usually suck. And on this year, of all years: Do not do them.' Well, he's a bundle of joy to blow away the clouds. I'll bet he's being just deluged with requests from his mates to join the fun on *Houseparty*. At a time when people need something to lift their spirits, Nate thinks we should cloak ourselves in sackcloth and ashes. Well, I for one disagree. So here are my top five April Fools jokes of all time. I am calling them by the rather snappy name of the *Nate Scott is a Wanker April Fool's Day Awards*.

5. THE SWISS SPAGHETTI HARVEST

In 1957, BBC news show Panorama announced that due to a mild winter and the elimination of the 'spaghetti weevil', farmers in Switzerland were enjoying a thriving spaghetti crop. Footage of Swiss farmers pulling strands of spaghetti down from trees was shown, and huge numbers of viewers calling the BBC up to ask how they could grow their own spaghetti tree. The BBC told viewers to, 'Place a sprig of spaghetti in a tin of tomato sauce and hope for the best'. The director-general of the BBC at the time even fell for this. At a time when you can't buy pasta in the shops, that would have been brilliant this year.

4. THE DECREASE OF GRAVITY

On April Fool's Day in 1976, the British astronomer Patrick Moore made an announcement during an early morning interview on BBC Radio 2 that, at precisely 9:47am the very same day, a once-in-a-lifetime astronomical event was going to occur. The planet of Pluto would pass behind Jupiter and this would then very briefly disrupt and lessen the Earth's own gravity. Moore told listeners that if they jumped in the air at precisely 9.47am, they would be able to float for a very short period of time. Scores of people called in excitedly claiming to have felt it, including at least one person who had apparently floated around the house before landing again. Though I think this was probably my friend Keith Howard on acid, so no great surprises there.

3. UFO LANDS IN LONDON

On March 31st 1989, the chairman of Virgin Records, Richard Branson, flew in a hot air balloon which had been specially designed to look like a UFO. Hundreds of motorists driving on the motorway outside London looked up to see what they thought was a glowing flying saucer descending into London. When the 'flying saucer' landed in a field on the outskirts of London, local residents called the police to inform them of an alien invasion. A police officer approached the 'spaceship' with his truncheon in hand, but ran in the opposite direction when the 'UFO' door opened and a silver-suited figure came out. I can only imagine how long he took to live that one down at the station. If it happened today, of course, they would have arrested Richard for being out on non-essential business and fined him the princely sum of thirty pounds. Which is still more than the Virgin Airlines staff will get this week.

2. EDISON'S MAGIC MACHINE

On 1st April 1878, the *New York Graphic* announced that Thomas Edison had invented an amazing new machine. The invention was said to turn water into wine, and earth into food. The patent office in Washington was besieged all day by crowds eager to learn the particulars of this amazing discovery. The great news was flashed all over the world, and literally dozens of newspapers published congratulatory leaders, paying tribute to Edison and to the wonderful world in which they now lived. I am guessing they weren't quite so glowing a couple of days later, when the Graphic published all of their headlines under the headline,

'They Bite'.

1. WW1 FOOTBALL 'BOMB'

And finally, my personal favourite. On April 1st 1915, a British aviator flying over Lille aerodrome in northern France dropped a 'bomb' on German troops. The bomb bounced to a great height - and continued bounding until finally coming to rest. After scrambling to take cover, the Germans warily went to examine the unexploded device, only to discover it was actually a football with the words 'April fool!' written on it.

Now that's how you have fun in a time of crisis, Nate lad!

2ND APRIL - WHAT DAY OF THE WEEK IS IT?

Am I the only person who is finding it hard to keep track of the days? Who is finding that, with all the normal activities which delineate and structure our lives disrupted, it is all morphing into one big virus-centric week? Now, I know people are still working at home, but the boundaries have decidedly blurred. There is no taking the children to school on weekdays. No football matches at the weekend. No Saturday night dinner party, or Sunday lunch at the pub. The signposts which map out our daily existence have been, if not uprooted, then at least had a sack popped over them for the time being. And, rather than freeing us up from the strictures of routine so we can look at the world with fresh eyes, that world has closed around each of us to just four walls - with just a digital connection out to a new and scarier world.

So, when I woke this morning, and checked to see what day it was on my phone, I got to wondering why we have seven days in the week in the first place, and how these days work. If it's Monday, for instance, why do we always have to wait five days until Saturday? And how come the day after Monday is Tuesday and not, say, Sunday? Now, I know you're probably thinking I've woken up all a bit addled after a few too many last night, but I will have none of it. I had two glasses of wine, watched TV with the boys, and was in bed at ten o'clock - only getting up about three hours later to tell them to turn off their bloody PS4s and go to sleep.

Anyway, it turns out it is all very interesting. The reason why we organize our lives around a seven-day week goes back to the Babylonians, who lived in what is now Iraq. They worked out that it takes the moon twenty-nine and a half days to cycle through all moon phases. But, having done this they figured that twenty-nine days seems quite a long period to organise things around - particularly as not many of them could get hold of a quill and some parchment to knock up a calendar for their fridge. So, they rounded the Moon cycle down to twenty-eight days, and divided this time span into four periods of seven days each, using leap days to stay in sync with the Moon phases in the longer term. Avid astronomers, the Babylonians assigned a day of the week to each of the classical planets - the seven non-fixed celestial bodies visible to the naked eye. These are: the Sun, the Moon, Mars, Mercury, Jupiter, Venus, and Saturn. The words we use for days of the week all derive from the Latin for these planets. But here it gets a bit strange; the Romans observed the speed at which the classical planets crossed the sky and concluded that the fastest object must have the shortest distance to the Earth, while the slowest object was believed to be farthest away, and they ordered the week based on this. The really odd, thing, however is that this would give the following sequence.

Saturn (Saturday)
Jupiter (Thursday)
Mars (Tuesday)
Sun (Sunday)
Venus (Friday)
Mercury (Wednesday)
Moon (Monday)

In other words, we would wake up after a big night out on a Saturday, and it would be Thursday morning, which would clearly mean bugger all got done at work on a Friday. Though Sunday night would be brilliant - rather than thinking the next day would be the first day of the working week, it would be Friday, and Monday morning blues would be eliminated at the stroke of a pen. So why do we have the order we have today? Well, those Romans were tricky blighters, they believed that each hour of the day was governed by one of the deities associated with the celestial bodies. According to them, the first hour of the first day of the week was thought to be governed by the Moon. Following the above order for each consecutive hour, the second hour was steered by Saturn, the third hour by Jupiter, and so on. By applying this pattern to all one hundred and sixty-eight hours of the week the Romans associated the first hour of each weekday with the following celestial bodies: Moon, Mars, Mercury, Jupiter, Venus, Saturn, Sun, Which, as the erudite amongst you will have worked out, equates to Monday, Tuesday, Wednesday and so on.

Why am I telling you all this? Well, the days of the week have come to have meanings associated with them which might not serve us in the new world if we go further on our current trajectory. We will need new words for the days. Words without the old connotations, which better reflect the new reality. After two thousand years the time for change is now, and you, readers are in the vanguard of this change. Below are my new day words. Try them out for size; take them out for a walk (though only once a day, obviously); see if you can improve upon them. But know that you are pioneers my friends - the final vanquishers of a Roman legacy which has passed down the eons through wars and famine. This is the start of a new tomorrow - or *Outsideday* as I now call it. Here is my new week.

Trumpday. This is the new start of the week day. But rather than that feeling of having to get up and get on the tube and go to work, we can replace it with the feeling we get when we switch on the TV and see the fat orange wanker about to open his mouth and lie to us.

Waitrose-day. This is the day when we're allowed to go shopping. Different communities will have their own colloquialism. In Chelsea, for instance, it will be known as *Harrodsday*, and in Newcastle as *Lidlday*. In Liverpool it will just be called *Robbingday*.

Corrieday. Given the difficulties filming, Coronation Street will now only be aired on TV once a week - much to the unbridled disappointment of the whole nation. Sadly too, there will be no shooting in the Rovers, the Bistro or Roy's Rolls. But the corner shop will stay open, as it provides an essential service, and rather than being thought the worst actor on TV, Dev Allahan will become a national hero, and a symbol for key workers up and down the country. With a fair wind, that ginger waste of space, Gary Windass, will be left isolating all by himself, and will be eventually forgotten and written out of the show.

Kloppday. As football will have become only a distant memory, and social distancing so engrained that people almost forget what it is liked to be hugged, *Kloppday* will be the day we remember the old world. The fabulous football, the wonderful fans, the great man hugging us all as the Mighty Reds stride towards a magnificent Premier League title - only for it to be snatched from their hands by an increasingly desperate Sir Alex Ferguson, shagging bats in a remote corner of China as his last resort to keep Liverpool from regaining their perch.

Wineday. Grape picking will be an occupation only for a few dedicated key-workers, and in the absence of the seasonal grape-picking workforce, most grapes will wither on the vine. This will lead to a massive increase in the cost of wine - so much so that it will be rationed to just two glasses per person, once a week. This will be distributed to us on *Wineday*, the last day of the working-at-home-week.

In-lawday. This is the old Saturday of course. You remember what feeling of freedom, when the whole weekend is waiting in front of you like an unexplored territory? Well, that will be long gone of course. Replaced instead with that wonderful knowledge that, since you are in now in splendid isolation, there is absolutely no chance at all that the bloody in-laws will pop over and ruin the weekend.

Nogodday. Religious sentiment will have risen in the early days of the pandemic, as it does in any crisis. But as time passes, and as there is no end in sight, all belief in an omniscient creator will have seeped away, and with it the religious differences and hatred that have separated us for millennia will evaporate like dew on a summer's morning. On *Nogodday* we will all take time out to think what life could have been like if we have never invented God in the first place. And we will all be happy, for one lovely, isolated moment.

3RD APRIL - FOOTBALLERS AND THEIR MONEY

Don't you just love footballers? Now, it's wrong to criticize someone who is doing some good - no matter how small. I know that. But this chap's a Manchester United player, so I'm going to. In 2018 Forbes reported that Paul Pogba was the fifth highest earning footballer on the planet, earning in excess of twenty million pounds a year. Which, by the standards of most of us, is a tidy sum, I think you will agree. It certainly pays for those one or two extra bits and pieces around the house, that's for sure. And maybe a curry on Saturday night. It has been estimated that Pogba's net worth may well be over a hundred million pounds. Which would pay for quite a few curries - even at the Vine and Spice, which is pretty expensive, as you probably know. His salary alone is two hundred and ninety thousand pounds a week. Regrettably - or not so regrettably, for those of us who can't stand the sight of the preening popinjay - Paul has been injured for most of the season. Indeed, he has only managed to play for five hundred and sixty minutes since the start of the season. Now, unlike most of us who are sick and can't go to work, his employer keeps on sending him sacksful of money week after week. Not his fault, I know, but a nice gig if you can get it. If you do the maths, this means that Pogba has actually been paid seventeen thousand pounds a minute for each minute he's been on the pitch i.e. for actually doing the job he gets paid for. Remember that number, it comes up later.

Why am I giving you chapter and verse on the Pogba finances? Well, the Manchester United midfielder has set up a fundraising page, and pledged financial support to UNICEF to help children affected by the virus. Pogba is also, apparently, hoping to provide disposable gloves, surgical masks and vented goggles for health workers through this fund, and he will double the value of the fund if its goal of twenty-seven thousand pounds is reached. Pogba said, 'The impact of a large-scale outbreak, especially on poor and vulnerable children, can be immense. It's my birthday and I'm always grateful that me, my family and friends are healthy. Nonetheless, not everybody is in good health right now. At times like this we need to come together.' Well happy birthday mate, but let me get this right. Provided other people who, on balance, are probably not worth a hundred mill', put up twenty-seven thousand pounds, you will then match this amount. That is almost two whole minutes of your actual earnings this season - about as long as it takes to sing an extended version of happy birthday. Or a fraction of the time you spend having your hair primped every bloody day. It's hardly Bill Gates, is it Paul?

But Pogba's minimalist largesse looks positively philanthropic compared with that of Tottenham Hotspur. Spurs, as you may have read, have furloughed all their non-playing staff - so the government now picks up the tab for eighty per cent of their wages. Let's assume that their two hundred and fifty staff earn an average of thirty-five thousand a year each, that equates to eight hundred thousand pounds a month that we, the taxpayer, will end up paying. Again, to give this some context, Harry Kane's salary alone is eight hundred thousand pounds a month. Tottenham's player wage bill, I am led to understand, is a hundred million pounds per annum. Or, around nine million a month. All that the bloated, overpaid prima donnas would need to do is sacrifice ten per cent of their salaries to fund the people who make their club tick. But they would much rather you and I fork this out - to support a club that hasn't actually won anything in living memory. and who has just paid over a billion pounds to build a flashy new stadium.

But footballers aren't all bad. There are good stories too, to balance out the rampant greed that charactersises much of the game. Wilfried Zaha already gives ten per cent of his Crystal Palace salary to charity, and he is stepping-up to help to ease the strain on the NHS during the coronavirus crisis. He apparently co-owns a property firm in London, and he's offering rent-free accommodation at fifty properties to health workers. Good on you Wilfried. If Robbie Fowler did the same, he could house the entire NHS in the North West I reckon. And, speaking of Merseyside, it was particularly nice to hear of one Premier League player (I'm not sure whether he was from Liverpool or Everton) who gave fifty thousand pounds to Alder Hay hospital, but requested anonymity rather than the oh-too-transparent virtue signaling of the likes of Pogba. Good on you. I'm pretty sure he wasn't from Everton.

And not all football clubs are avaricious either. Here's a shout-out for Stockport County. The decision to suspend football fixtures during the outbreak has left a lot of non-league clubs financially vulnerable, but Stockport have still tried to help. The National League side have donated seventy-five thousand pounds to Stockport NHS Foundation Trust to help pay for equipment which will treat patients with severe symptoms. The club's owner, Mark Stott, said, 'Stockport is a town and club with enormous community spirit and we'll support each other at this difficult time. Unfortunately, many people within the Stockport area will be affected by coronavirus and we wish them a speedy recovery. The NHS do a phenomenal job and on behalf of myself, the club and the supporters we would like to thank them for their selfless work during this unprecedented time.'

Just to put this into context. The average cost of a ticket to see Stockport is fifteen pounds, at Spurs it is closer to fifty. The average gate at Stockport is four thousand, compared with sixty thousand at Spurs. And it is certainly some time since Stockport had a multi-million-pound windfall from a trip to a Champions League final. Though I am sure most of you, given Spurs quite appalling parsimony, will now be delighted that that was a final which saw Spurs well and truly beaten by an infinitely better and more loveable opponent.

4TH APRIL - KEY WORKERS

'Key-workers' is a term that has penetrated the public consciousness in recent days with the speed and ferocity of a Steven Gerrard free-kick. I start with this simile as I know it will raise a smile from my good friend Brendan in California, who is ceaselessly amazed at my ability to reference the current World and European champions in everything I write, no matter how unrelated, and will be agog I have now achieved this in my very first sentence. Brendan, some of you may recall was my virtual friend on my blog, *Watching the River Flow* - the Facebook page for which, by the way, is still very much available to those of you who can't get enough of reading my nonsense. Brendan lives in a place called Eureka, which is a term which I am sure we all hope we hear pretty damn soon to replace any of the coronavirus lingua franca. Anyhow, unlike 'containment stage', 'key-workers' looks like it's settled in for the duration. We applaud them. We revere them. We praise them.

Very possible, we may, from a suitably safe distance, even fancy them. Whatever our reaction, this crisis has certainly focused our attention on their importance in keeping the wheels of our society from falling off altogether. A list of some of these key-workers is quite interesting: nurses, delivery drivers, shop check-out girls (this isn't misogynistic, it's just my age unfortunately), utility workers, undertakers. This is by no means exhaustive, but in some ways the list of non-key-workers makes more interesting reading: bankers, options traders, most manufacturers, teachers, publicans, traffic wardens, management consultants. accountants, pointless celebrities, sportsmen (and women!), marketing people, me. At a time of crisis, when I'm guessing most of us would like to think we can do something useful, the huge majority of us appear to have zero value. We're the ones stuck at home, doing bugger all other than using copious quantities of toilet roll and getting pissed. Very often at the same time I suspect. Which gets you thinking, really - what effect will all this isolation, and time to think, have on our view of the world when we emerge from isolation blinking into the new sunlight.

Going back in time a few millennia, probably the most famous self-isolator in history was Moses. For those of you who didn't concentrate in your RE lessons at school, Moses led his people out of slavery in Egypt. Six weeks after they had surprised their pursuers by parting the Red Sea, Moses and his merry band of Israelites rocked up at Mount Sinai and set up camp. But, hardly had they got their tent pegs in, than God started prattling on to them about a bunch of new rules. Now, I am guessing most of them had pretty well had it with God by then - what with all those bloody plagues and all - and were far keener on having a bit of fun to celebrate their new found liberty than listen to the omnipotent one. So, after hearing the first couple of commandments, they switched up the beat-box and pretty much ignored him. You can probably speculate how they felt. Imagine how you would feel if you had just got out of prison and Piers Morgan popped up and started telling you what to do .... that would the mindset of the average Israelite. So Moses, who was a bit hacked off with this development as he could see his authority on the wane, threw a bit of a strop and buggered off up Mount Sinai. And stayed there for forty days, reflecting on life, while the people waiting below had a knees-up. During this time, our boy didn't eat or drink as, apparently, the supermarket supply chain had broken down, so he took to chiseling out God's full set of commandments on a couple of tablets of stone to pass the time, and take the edge off the whole hunger and thirst thing. Why am I rambling on about Moses I hear you ask? Well, it seems to me there is a sporting chance that each of us 'non-essentials' may well be locked away for forty days as well, and one of the things many of us may just reflect upon is whether, in the great scheme of things, what they do is essential or not, and what the big picture really looks like for them?

When I was growing up there was a TV programme called *Tomorrow's World*, which almost everyone used to watch. Mainly because it was just before *Top of the Pops*, but it was still better than whatever was on ITV at the time. We called them 'programmes' rather than 'shows' in those days, of course, as we hadn't been totally overwhelmed by the vacuity of American culture. The purpose of *Tomorrow's World* was to tell us of new developments in science and technology - not about the here and now, necessarily, but about what things would be like in the future as different technologies took hold. A 1967 episode of *Tomorrow's World*, for instance, glimpsed at a future where computers would be a fixture in our homes and workplaces. Mobile phones made their first appearance on the show (alright, I get it, I've become Americanised!) in 1979. A show, in 1994, talked of the infinite possibilities of the 'Information Superhighway'. I remember to this day being regaled at the innovations they announced - that seem so ordinary now, but so incredible back then: the fax, the home computer, the compact disc, the phonecard, the CAT scanner, the pocket calculator, the personal stereo, the disposable camera, suspenderless stockings' (or 'tights' as we know them now). The emphasis of the show was that science would bring about a better and easier world for all of us (although I imagine lots of blokes would probably disagree about the whole tights thing), but Tomorrow's World couldn't get it right every time, could they? The thrust was that science would make the world a better, a more enjoyable place. Now, it's hard to disagree that science has not delivered in spades over the last fifty years. I am typing this essay on a laptop computer that has massively more processing power than was needed to put man on the moon. Somehow or other, without even being plugged in, I have access to all the world's knowledge and entertainment at the push of a button. I can call up my friends anywhere in the world, and even see them on my screen. Moses would be thrilled to know how easy it is to find out all about him, that I can research his desert wandering to my heart's content without ever leaving my bedroom.. He would, of course, give all the plaudits to God, and be far less pleased that I regularly break the Big Man's commandments, but hey, you can't have everything, old timer! So why, given that technology has, if anything, over delivered, is life far from easier or happier for a great many of us? One of the axioms of *Tomorrow's World* was that it spoke to a better world; a happier world. A world where people would need to work less, have more free time in which to enjoy and better themselves; where automation would take away the routine and the mundane. So why, then, are so many of us today fundamentally unhappy? Why do so many people dread the daily grind? Why is life so much more, rather than less, stressful? And why, for all the hard work so many of us put into acquiring and progressing in their careers, do so many feel 'non-essential'?

Well, one answer might be that technology itself is to blame. With advances in technology, with instant access to information, and with the ability to compare pricing instantaneously and easily, has come an explosion in competitiveness. Conventional capitalist wisdom would say this as a good thing - that it drives down pricing, fosters ingenuity, and leads to better cheaper product, which is more affordable and enhances their lives of the many. All of which is true of course, but with this comes some big unintended consequences. It creates a climate of intensity, and a level of stress and anxiety, that feeds through organisations like a virus. A three-year study by ADP found that three key measures of employee wellbeing - optimism, stress and skills confidence - have taken a big hit since 2015. Whilst the exact reason for the changes was unclear, there was a clear suggestion that the rise in new technologies entering the workplace was a key driver. In 2018, money and work were the top two sources of stress, according to the American Psychological Association. In a recent survey, over two thousand professionals told Korn Ferry that they are more stressed than five years ago - with two-thirds saying it's costing them sleep - and they cited the key causative factors as keeping up with changes in technology and increased workloads. So, it would appear that all that technology, that was supposed to make our life easier, may actually be having the reverse effect.

But it seems wrong to blame technology itself - after all, it's not the tools at our disposal that shape our outcomes, but what we choose do with them. So, where then does the problem lie? I go back to a point I made in an earlier essay. Year-on-year growth is simply unsustainable - and completely illogical as a central axiom to run this world of ours. If we add into the mix the fact that prices generally are being driven down by the new technologies, the underlying reality is that we are defining ourselves - and ordering our world - by growth objectives which are even worse than they seem at first sight. And, as automation and technology increases, the requirement for us all to pedal faster on our hamster wheels increases rather than decreases. I am guessing that many of us - particularly those on the non-essential list - may well use our forty days in the desert to question whether this game really is worth the candle!

5TH APRIL - CELEBRITIES AND THEIR KIDS

For some reason my attention this morning was drawn to an article in the online Daily Mirror entitled: *Gwyneth Paltrow shares best vibrators to use during the Coronavirus lockdown*. I can't think why. I imagine, however, that Gwyneth first got into extensive vibrator use when married to *Coldplay* frontman, Chris Martin - in order to keep her awake, as well as distracting her from the appalling racket coming out of his mouth. Anyhow, much though I tried to resist, I couldn't help but read the article, and learned a couple of quite astonishing things about La Paltrow. Firstly, she is wont to give all manner of advice to people via her health and wellness advice brand, *Goop*, including, apparently, some words of wisdom on vaginal steaming. Now, call me naive if you will, but I'd never heard of vaginal steaming. So, I looked it up on the internet (before promptly deleting my history of course), and was astonished to find out that this involves squatting over a bowl of hot water laced with herbs, and letting the steamy delights waft upwards. I was even more astonished to find a picture of model, Chrissy Teigan actually doing this, with a blanket on her knees and, rather disturbingly, wearing a face-pack. What would possess Chrissy to do post this on *Instagram* is beyond me. And what would possess nine hundred and seventy thousand one hundred and eight-four people to 'like' it is so far beyond me I am at a complete loss for words.

Anyhow, I am straying from Gwyneth now. The second thing I learned about her is that she and Chris named their daughter 'Apple' - one can only hope that particular Apple fell as far from the tree as it possibly could. And avoided the vaginal steaming pot on her way down. But it got me to thinking about the ridiculous names celebrities like to call their children. 'Apple', as it happens, struggles to get anywhere near the top 10. Jay Z and Beyoncé, for instance, called their little bundle of egotistical joy, 'Blue Ivy'. Kate Winslet's little one is called 'Bear Blaze' - though, as the father is some chap called Ned Rocknroll, this does start to make some sort of deranged sense. Though they are all put to shame by Frank Zappa, who called his three kids: 'Moon Unit', 'Dweezil', and 'Diva Thin Muffin'. I am pretty sure they never got bullied at school.

The thing about Johnny and Jemima Celeb, clearly, is that, as their self-conception is one of their vast importance and uniqueness in the universe, it is inconceivable that they would settle for naming their offspring anything remotely ordinary. They would want a name that served as a symbol for their own individuality and exceptionality. But, for the true celebrity couple, this is a tricky business indeed. The name cannot be seen to be closer to one celeb's name or persona than their partner, as this would clearly tilt their personal celebrity axis, and be a beacon to the world to illuminate which of the two was the more 'A' list. So, I got to thinking how this intractable problem might be solved for different celebs, where they ever to get it on together - how they could take a little bit of each of their names, and come up with a combo that reassured the world of their joint status, but still came up with a name of individuality and panache. If Pricilla Presley got it together with Rick Astley, for instance, they could call their son 'Prick'. That's the 'P' from 'Priscilla' and the 'Rick' from … well you are probably getting it I think. Here, in no particular order, are some of my other favourites:

Debby Harry/Don Johnson:	**Hardon**
Lady Gaga/Gary Barlow:	**GaGaGaBa**
Sonny Bono/Cher:	**Boner**
Sting/Fi Glover:	**Stifi**
Michael Hutchence/Brooke Shields:	**Choke** (which is sort of ironic really.)
P. Diddy/Samantha Fox:	**Pox** or even **Poxy**, if they are feeling particularly affectionate.
Courtney Cox/Ronaldo:	**Corona**. As Kevin Keegan once said, 'I would just love it'.

And this is not just the province of the straight couple. Imaginary gay couplings can equally have fun naming their adopted fashion accessories:

Tammy Wynette/Angela Rippon:	**Tampon** She could happily play with Tammy's adopted daughter

from her relationship with Lily Allen, **Lilette**.

Michael Jackson/Boris Karloff: **Jackoff**.

MC Hammer/King George VI: **Stammer** I can just see their little one in years to come giving us a rendition of *Stammertime*. It would take about an hour.

J-Lo/Twiggy: **Jiggy** In fairness, I would definitely fork out a tenner to see those two actually making jiggy.

Boris Johnson/Ingmar Bergman: **Boring** Though this would be a tough one, as Ingmar's dead. And Boris isn't looking too sharp right now either.

And finally, for the man who loves himself so much he needs no partner, just some hot self-loving:

Sylvester Stallone: **Slyone**

You can play too. Feel free to post your favourite celebrity-coupling-offspring-names as comments. Have fun and stay safe, and if you're thinking of going outside, as Donna Summer and Mr. T said when they named their little one, ***Don't***.

6TH APRIL - MEET THE NEW BOSS

I see that the Labour party has appointed Sir Keir Starmer as its new leader. Now, it has to be a good thing that we won't have to put up with old PLO-loving weasel-face any more, but it would have been nice if Keir had got off to a slightly better start. The knee-jerk response of the modern politician is to criticise first and ask questions later, and regrettably Labour's new incumbent seems to have grasped this baton on day one. Virtually his first action after his election, as he looked to grab our attention at a time when none of us is the least interested in party politics, was to tell us that the Prime Minister has made 'serious mistakes' in his response to the ongoing pandemic. In an article for *The*

Sunday Times, on his first full day as party leader, he said: 'The public is placing an enormous trust in the government at the moment: it is vital that that trust is met with openness and transparency about those mistakes and the decisions that have been made.'

He went on to say that we were 'far behind on testing', that frontline workers couldn't get protective equipment due to 'blockages in the system', and that 'the government must listen to our frontline NHS and care workers'. Well we all do know where we are right now, Kier, we watch the news. But at a time like this don't people want to see unity? They want our leaders to point in the same direction, not go in for petty point scoring. I am absolutely sure the government have made mistakes - people make mistakes in a war, particularly when they are being overrun by the enemy. Bickering about them when the bullets are still flying, however, seems rather counterproductive - and more than a tiny bit demoralising for the population at large who are, I would imagine, less likely to have trust in what the government are doing, and less likely to support and abide by government decisions. All at a time when trust is pretty essential. Mr. Starmer didn't enlighten us on what the wrong decisions were - or what he would have done differently - but then again, it's always easy to criticise the people who have to actually make decisions when you are standing on the side-lines.

What we also don't want to see is people making political capital out of this crisis in order to reinforce their own agendas. Kier immediately latched onto the fact that we have seen the importance of our key-workers to tell us how they all should be paid more, and that the 'wealthy' should do the paying. Right or wrong, now is not the time to start electioneering, Kier, it's the time to look at what you can do for your country. Maybe I'm unfairly focusing on the new Labour leader - he's just been elected, and I get he wants to make a bit of a rattle so this fact doesn't bypass us completely. But it's depressing that all politicians seem the same. They all believe that, only by them being in power, will the world become a better place - so their raison d'être is to get elected at all costs in order to implement their policies and ideas. Well, whilst the role of the opposition is certainly to challenge the government of the day and hold it to account, should it not equally be to support the right decisions at the right time? And are we not all fed up to the back teeth with platitudes, soundbites, and blatant over-simplifications from all sides of politics?

Take the NHS. Much is being made of the need for better funding and, having delivered services to the NHS for thirty years, it is hard not to argue that this is true in many respects. But the line in argument that its problems responding to this pandemic are rooted in underfunding and austerity is just wrong and unhelpful. The French spend a whopping twenty-five per cent more on healthcare per head than we do, but their health service is creaking in similar ways to our own. The reason the NHS - and health authorities the world over - can't cope, is the sheer overload of patients being condensed into a short space of time. We have war-time, not peace-time conditions. If we had invested huge amounts of additional capital into the NHS, there is no way that would have been spent having forty thousand ventilators hanging around, for instance, when the normal requirement is only for four thousand. This would have been seen as a ludicrous use of public funds.

No, the problem here lies not with any one government's investment decisions, but in the abdication of successive governments of their first duty - that of protecting the citizens of this country. The SARS outbreak of 2003 gave the world a taster of what might happen with a viral pandemic - but we were lucky then - the virus didn't transmit nearly as quickly as coronavirus, so the spread was able to be contained with only relatively little human cost. It wouldn't have been a huge leap, however, for the government at the time - or indeed world governments acting collectively - to have asked themselves the question of what might have happened if SARS had been transmitted easier and faster. And to then put in place contingency plans in the event of the emergence of a more rapidly spreading virus - and to fund this through our defence budget. Then, maybe, we might have stockpiles of the tools we need to fight this war against this unseen enemy - in the same way as we have stockpiles of weapons to fight potential human enemies. Just a thought. Though, clearly not one that Jeremy Corbyn had when his trade union mate foretold all of this to him ten years ago.

As an aside, for those of you who read my post yesterday, if Boris Johnson and Keir Starmer were to come out of the cupboard and adopt a little one, they could call it **Joke**. Which would be quite funny. And if Diane Abbot and Jeremy Corbyn got it together (which they purportedly did) they would call it … well I can't think to be honest - I'm too busy poking red hot needles into my eyes lest someone ever showed me the video.

7th April - Shocking!

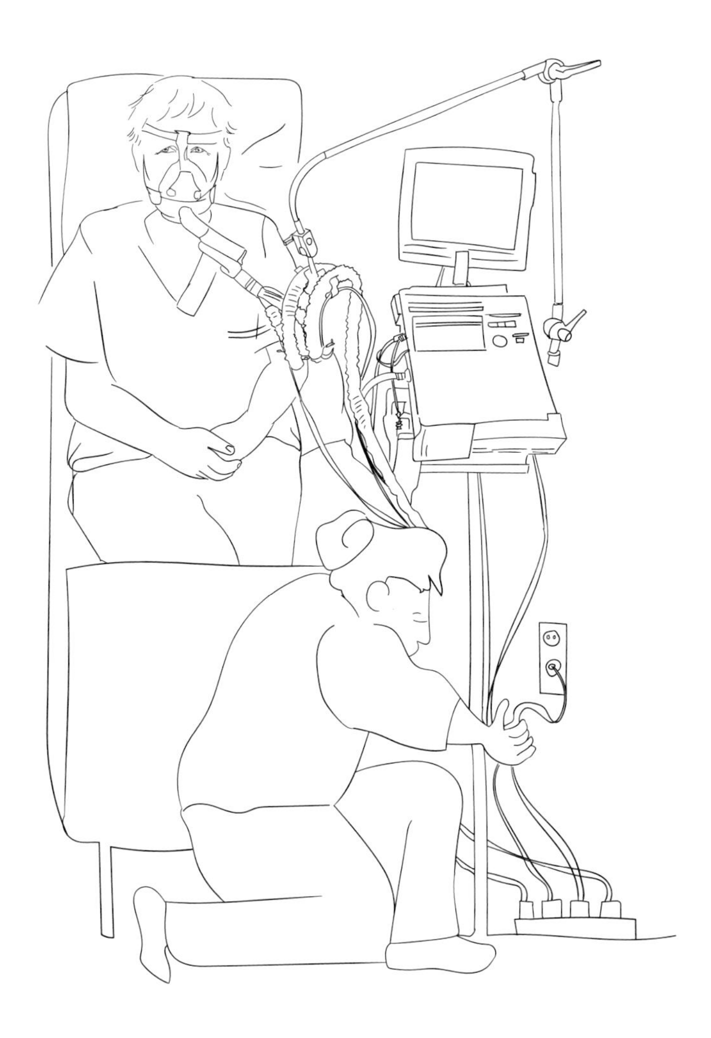

Now, I'm not easily shocked, but this has been a shocking couple of days. First came the quite awful news that Liverpool FC were furloughing some of their staff - whilst at the same time still paying the likes of Virgil Van Dyke ten millions pounds a year. Only the Heysel stadium disaster left me feeling so ashamed to be a Liverpool fan - and that was more fan-related than club-related. Having criticised Spurs on this post so lavishly a few days ago, it is hard to not level exactly the same insults at my club. And that hurts. If there is a redeeming grace, it is that there was a massive backlash from fan and ex-players alike, who could see what an awful decision this was, and the club quickly reversed the decision. But all the goodwill generated by Jurgen Klopp and the players leading the support of the NHS, and by Jordan Henderson leading the efforts of football captains across the Premier league to establish and contribute to a supporting fund, has been well and truly eclipsed. Sad.

But infinitely more shocking was the Facebook post by the Mayor of Heaner (which is in Derbyshire, for the Southerners amongst you), one Sheila Oates. When hearing that Boris had been admitted into intensive care, she posted:

Sorry, he completely deserves this and he is one of the worst PMs we have ever had.

It is hard to think of a more heartless and unpleasant thing to do or say. The Labour council, all credit to them, were horrified, and withdrew the whip immediately. But it got me wondering what Sheila was like - what kind of person makes so horrendous and unempathetic a comment about a man - the leader of our country, whether you like him or not - who is seriously ill in hospital, and has a family and a pregnant fiancée. To be so callous, she strikes me as someone with something of the Donald Trump in her, I mused. Well, one look at her picture makes you pretty damn sure she would never have anything of the actual Trump inside her - she's definitely not the kind of chick Donald would be marching over and grabbing by the pussy, that's for sure. Less Stormy Daniels, more Never-gets-her Oates I reckon. They must have been worried they would have to invest in a few extra links on the mayoral chain when they popped it over her head. Am I being unfair and body-prejudiced? Probably, but if this ghastly woman doesn't deserve it, who does?

Anyhow, I thought I would delve a bit deeper into Ms. Oates and see what I could find about her. It turns out that she studied Law at Nottingham Trent University - and you will know my view on lawyers from my previous posts. She is also - and hold your breath Donald - single. She professes herself 'interested in men', however - though not public-school educated ones with blond foppish hair, I am guessing - and supports Sheffield United. I can only imagine the joy of seeing her pulling on that red and white Blades footie shirt. Phew! She numbers, amongst her favourite films, *LethalWeapon and A Matter of life and Death* - which is pleasingly ironic in its own way I suppose - and lists her favourite TV show as *Thunderbirds are Go*. I quite liked the Thunderbirds when I was seven, but I'm not sure I would want to be voting anyone Mayor who still like them at fifty-one, if I'm honest (I could be being generous with the fifty-one I reckon). She also likes *Toohunky Toys*. I had to look this up, but now I have, there is definitely something of the *Spongebob Square Pants* about that head of hers. More tellingly, perhaps, she lists as a 'like': *The England Leeds Mission - The Church of Latter-day Saints*.

I never imagined I would ever look at a religious site, but I was moved to check out the website for *The England Leeds Mission - The Church of Latter-day Saints*. The first thing that astonished me was that, after the picture of a handsome looking Jesus, you scroll down to a quite stunning looking girl promoting their Twitter feed. This girl looks nothing like Sheila at all. One look at her over a crowded room and the Donald would be already instructing his lawyers to draw up settlement and gagging contracts. Sex sells, it would appear, even when you've got God on your side. The next scroll down is to some religious stuff, where we can find out about 'Holy Week: Day by Day'. I am guessing that they don't finish on Nogodday. (If you don't understand that you haven't been reading my posts assiduously enough. Keep Up!). But then, bugger me, they then go right back into shameless sexploitation, as we are encouraged to 'Talk with Missionaries Online' against a backdrop picture of a couple of young stunners who look like they danced at the same top Ibiza nightclub as the Twitter Girl. Bizarre. Not sure I will try it though - one imagines that it is a bit like a telephone sex line, and, rather than the hottie on the advert you think you are talking to, you get Sheila whispering sweet nothings down the telephone in her Blackburn accent, whilst wearing her footie shirt and yanking her mayoral chain. At the end of the page we are enticed to, 'Learn what it means to be more of a community and how it can help us to all look out for each other.' as well as extolling the fact that, 'What we preach on a Sunday we try to practice every day.' Though I'm pretty sure Sheila never made it down that far, judging by the empathy of her tweets.

8th April - Harry and Meghan

It is with great restraint that I avoid breaking the keys on my laptop. But in a world that includes Donald Trump and Sheila (never-gets-any) Oates, incredibly the Sussexes - or whatever name they give themselves these days - have made it to the top of my 'really-really-bleedin'-hate-them list'. And that's quite an achievement.

The Duke and Duchess of Sussex chose this week to announce to the Telegraph what wonderful and charitable people they were, and how they have drawn up proposals for a vast and selfless array of projects under the name 'Archewell'. This apparently includes running emotional support groups, a multi-media educational empire, and even launching a wellbeing website. They were originally going to call this project 'SussexRoyal', until the Queen told them to go and take a hike, as they are now no longer Royals, but this didn't stop the Sussexes gushing about their substitute name: 'Before SussexRoyal came the idea of 'Arche' - the Greek word meaning 'source of action'. We connected to this concept for the charitable organisation we hoped to build one day, and it became the inspiration for our son's name. Archewell is a name that combines an ancient word for strength and action, and another that evokes the deep resources we each must draw upon.'

Now, apart from being quite vomit-inducingly Californian, on a scale of one to ten, how much do we really think that, when looking to name their impending bundle of joy, they sat down and thought, 'I know, what's the Greek word for 'source of action.' - that would be perfect for our little chap? And do you really think that they are, 'connected to this concept', for the charitable organisation they hoped to build one day, and it became the inspiration for their son's name as they would have us believe? Because if that's true, little Archie must have turned out to be a right little shit, as they immediately dumped him and changed the name to SussexRoyal - only to then, and quite shamelessly, come back to using Archie when Plan A went out of the window.

Now, I don't want to be over critical. In fairness to the Sussexes, they weren't actually using the day that the death toll in the UK reached its highest so far as their preferred date to launch Archewell. Even they are not deluded enough to think this would make much of a splash, given everything else that's going on. Their reason for chatting away to The Telegraph was, and I quote, 'Like you, our focus is on supporting efforts to tackle the global Covid-19 pandemic but faced with this information coming to light, we felt compelled to share the story of how this came to be.'

So, what they were doing was putting down a place-holder, if you will. Making sure they actually stayed in the news. A bit like when they give little insights and snippets to get us excited before the big launch of a James Bond movie. The Bond parallel breaks down a bit, though, as there is no way they are ever going to have a balding ginger Bond - although I'm absolutely sure Meghan thinks she would make a fabulous bond girl. She would need to be called something appropriately exotic. Pussy Manure, maybe.

And what, pray, are the loved-up twosome doing with regard to, 'Supporting efforts to tackle the global Covoid-19 pandemic?' Building ventilators? Writing to the families of victims? Donating money to the NHS? Shutting the fuck up? Well, funnily enough, house-hunting in Malibu wouldn't be the first thing that leapt to mind - but it's a tough life for an ex-royal, I guess, though someone's got to do it. Still, it's nice and quiet out in Malibu right now, what with all the fans and celeb hunters in lockdown.The only thing to disturb the solitude they seem to so crave will be the gentle hum of Gwyneth Paltrow's vibrator wafting over the back fence.

During the Blitz, the King and Queen refused to leave London, and visited bombed areas to see the damage caused by enemy air raids. On these visits, the Queen took a keen interest in what was being done to help people who had lost their homes. After Buckingham Palace was bombed, on 13th September 1940, she said she felt she could, 'Look the East End in the face.' She must be turning over in her grave looking down on her great-grandson today. Oh wait! 'Is he actually her grandson at all?' I hear you ask!

9TH APRIL - THE CORONAVIRUS CASUALS

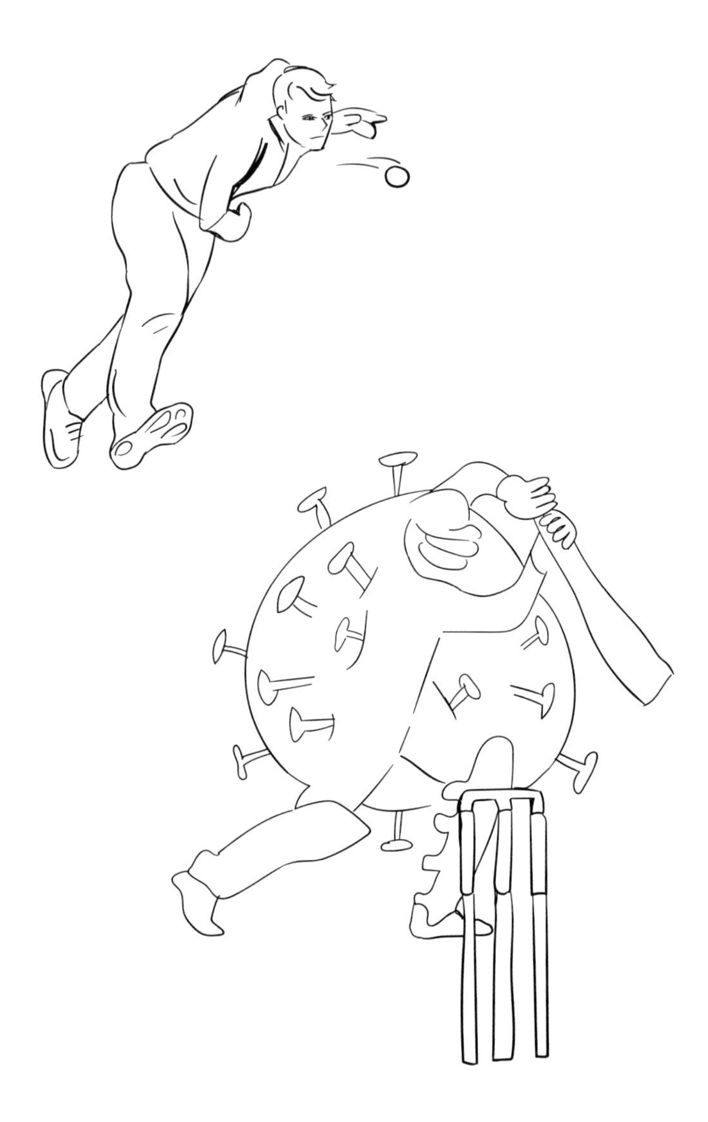

I spotted a news piece on the internet this morning about the police coming across twenty or thirty blokes who were playing cricket in Kensal Green. That's shocking, and really hard to believe. Who'd have thought they played a proper game like cricket in a place like Kensal

Green? Anyhow, as you might imagine, these morons ran off when they saw the Old Bill. The police didn't catch any of them - other than one of the batsmen who decided to come back for a chancy second, I believe. I hear the police fined him half his match fee. Idiots though these people clearly are, particularly on a beautiful day like today, it got me wondering when we might next hear the sound of leather on willow floating across from the Green on a Sunday afternoon. And when I would next hike halfway across the county on a drizzly Wednesday to see one of my boys charge down the wicket and get out first ball. It's amazing the things you miss. On the flip side though, England haven't lost a test match for ages, so that's definitely an unexpected bonus. Getting to think about cricket, however, did, oddly, get me wondering where many of the people making the news in these coronovirus days might be fielding were we to play a game against this stroppy virus to settle our differences. So here is my team, and their fielding positions, for the clash between the deadly Wuhan Wanderers and the brave Coronavirus Casuals.

Wicketkeeper and captain. This clearly has to be Chief Medical Officer, Chris Whitty, who seems like the kind of absolutely top bloke we want in such an important position. Apparently his dad was murdered by PLO terrorists in Athens, so a bloody good job that toe-rag Jeremy Corbyn isn't PM right now - it's hard to think they would share the same beliefs about freedom fighters.

First slip. I'm going to put Boris at first slip. Cleary he doesn't look too mobile on his pins (particularly at the moment), so he's a natural candidate for first slip anyhow, but I think it's fair to say he made the first slip position his own with his pretty muted and slow response to the outbreak. That's not me being allYvette Copper about it, and demanding answers and passing blame, it's just a fact he would probably 'fess up to in a quiet moment. Since then I think he's been pretty good though, so he deserves his place in the team. I'm hoping he doesn't let any balls through and have to run down to Third Man, though, as dragging that oxygen machine with him will really slow things up.

Fine Leg. Only one choice for this, the vibrator queen herself, Gwyneth Paltrow, who has very fine legs indeed, I seem to recall. And given the quality of the wicketkeeper, she won't have much to do, so she will be able to pleasure herself to her heart's content - and be first into the clubhouse to get an extra helping of the lovely love-eggs salad.

Silly mid-off: Mike Pence. Mike Pence is a very silly man indeed. This doesn't in any way make him unique in the Trump administration, but Mike is a religious nutjob who believes in Armageddon and a final conflagration in which the righteous will vanquish the wicked. Which is perhaps slightly further on than 'silly' on the spectrum. Some people have been known to wonder why no-one has tried to assassinate Trump - but look at Mike, you know the answer; the alternative is even worse. It's a traditional thing in cricket - when you put people at silly mid-off you normally tell them it's because they are really sharp in the field. The main reasons, though, are either that they're pretty dispensable in the great scheme of things, or that seeing them take a drive full in the nuts would be rather fun, as they've irritated the hell out of you. Both are definitely true about Pence. Though for his sake, let's hope he doesn't get carried off after he's been hit. Heaven forbid he's alone in the clubhouse sharing love eggs with Gwyneth - his religious beliefs mean he's never allowed to eat alone with a woman other than his wife. Particularly one with such cracking legs.

Square leg. This has got to be the ubiquitous Sheila Oates. If her legs are anything like her head, then I am guessing they are very square indeed.

Slips 2-5. These are all filled by Donald Trump. Clearly this is a man who can slip up without even blinking, so I'm giving him a lot of slip space to strut his stuff. But, even though I'm a bit worried about that hair getting in those beady eyes of his, I am quietly confident that he will be a beautiful slip fielder, and that he will do a great job for us. An outstanding job in fact. Indeed, all of the other cricketers have been astonished at how quickly he's picked up the game. And he's already the most popular cricketer the world has ever seen, so he's definitely our trump card. There was a scurrilous rumour that Donald had actually completely dropped the ball in this crisis, but I can categorically confirm that that was fake news, put about by the deep state, the media, and the MCC.

At Cover, I'm going for Meghan Markle. You can't deny her ability to give us lots of coverage - and she will be able to give emotional wellness sessions during the drinks break, which we're all really looking forward to. Particularly The Donald, who I heard muttering something about grabbing her fanny. My only concern is of her of drifting out of position - one bit of criticism from the fans and she'll be off over the other side of the field before you can say, 'Malibu Beach-house'.

If you get the one, you get the other, so, at Extra Cover, we have The-Cricketer-Formerly-Known-As-Prince-Harry. Now, I know he's a complete waste of space, but at least we've got someone to hold Meghan's hand and polish her box. Besides, I'm good mates with his Dad - we were in the cavalry together. Allegedly.

I'm going for little Johnny Bercow at short mid-wicket. We need a gobby sod in that position to give those virus boys a bit of sledging, and Johnny's just the chap. Besides he's got bugger all to do now some bird has got his job. And he must have a bloody good publisher, as he got his book out faster than England's middle order in an Ashes Test, so I thought I could have a bit of a chat to him in the drinks break to see if I can get some tips from the little fellow.

Point. That's me of course. Why? Because if I wasn't there, there would be no point at all.

And finally, the bowler. These Wuhan boys are good - there's no way they're going to get out to the short stuff. Anything close to the head and they'll be all over us like a rash. No, we need a top spinner. And there is no better in the game than the spin-master general, 'Call-me-Tony' Blair. Call-me-Tony has the full spinner's repertoire:

The wrong 'un: 'This pandemic clearly originates in Iraq, where they have been harbouring viruses of mass destruction now for many years'.

The Chinaman: 'China has done an extraordinary job of mobilising since the spread of the coronavirus'.

The flipper: 'But I wouldn't accept that the Chinese system, in that sense, is superior'.

The straight one: 'There are a lot of lessons to be learnt about global coordination, but in the short term we have to follow the scientific advice.'

Let's face it, any man who can bomb the shit out of the Arabs, and then get the job as Middle East Peace Envoy, is the kind of slippery chap we need to winkle out these nasty foreign virus jonnies on a sticky wicket like the one we're on today.

Anyhow, I'm off. We won the toss, and we're batting, so I need to put on the old PPE equipment.

10TH APRIL - IT'S JUST NOT CRICKET

It's really hard to warm to politicians. Pretty well any of them really. They're all delighted to take the credit for just about anything, but not too keen at all on taking the flak when they've stuffed up. And there is nothing more that they love than taking advantage of a problem or a crisis for their own ends; no situation is too sacred to not exploit to further an agenda. Frankly, they're just not gentlemen. Cricket, on the other hand, has always been the pastime of the gentleman. A game played with passion, but with honesty and integrity. Australians apart, obviously. So, following my theme from yesterday, today I announce my *It's-just-not-cricket XI*. They will take on the winners of yesterday's game, who will almost certainly be the Wuhan Wanderers, I fear, but I have no doubt that they will cheat, kill, bribe, lie and spin their way to a memorable victory.

First up is Governor Andrew Cuomo of New York. At a press conference on Thursday Cuomo told us, 'This is tremendously disruptive on all sorts of levels. It came out of the blue. For me, in New York, it reminds me of 9/11 where one moment which was inconceivable just changed everything. It changed your perspective on the world, it changed your perspective on safety... We've lost over 7,000 lives to this crisis. That is so shocking and painful and breathtaking, I don't even have the words for it. There was no explosion, but it was a silent explosion that just ripples through society with the same randomness, the same evil that we saw on 9/11.'

Now I have sympathy for Cuomo, having to deal with the shocking state of affairs in New York right now. He has a nightmare on his hands, as New York, a state of just twenty million people, is worse affected than any entire country in the world. But, apart from lots of people dying quite quickly, it's really not at all like 9/11, is it Andrew? 9/11 was indeed a shock - no-one could really have expected to see airplanes being catapulted into the Twin Towers, but this pandemic thing was entirely predictable. Bill Gates foresaw it in his TED talk in 2015. Barack Obama, in a speech to the Senate in 2005, said, 'The failure to prepare for emergencies can have devastating consequences. We learned that lesson the hard way after Hurricane Katrina. This nation must not be caught off-guard when faced with the prospect of an avian flu pandemic. The consequences are too high. The question is will we be ready when that happens? Let's make sure that answer is yes. I urge my colleagues in the Senate and the House to push this Administration to take the action needed to prevent a catastrophe that we have not seen during our lifetimes.'

Cuomo has been in the job for nine years now. Long enough to get it. Man-up mate, you're part of the problem here.

Opening the batting with Cuomo is, of course, The Donald. What a beautiful batsman. The most beautiful batsman since that other Don - who had such a beautiful name. But more perfect. And more popular. Every day Trump does or says something to guarantee his position in the team, but, I will just pick one Trump pearl from its shell at random to justify his inclusion. In 2015 the Obama Administration set up the *White House National Security Council Directorate for Global Health Security and Biodefense* to prepare for future pandemics - like COVID-19. In 2018, Donald Trump eliminated it, and with it much of the planning and preparedness went out of the window. Trump dismissed criticism that disbanding the team had slowed things down, calling it a 'nasty question' at a White House briefing, and saying that, 'I don't know anything about it'. If this boy can't make a hundred on a turning wicket, nobody can!

First wicket down, and we're going to a country not renowned for its cricketing prowess: Hungary. That is, of course, if you exclude my younger son, who took six wickets for one run in a two-over spell last season - including a hattrick, I'll have you know. But my pick isn't anyone so close to home; I am selecting Hungarian Prime Minister, Viktor Orban. In the name of combating the coronavirus pandemic. the Hungarian Parliament has given Orban the right to rule indefinitely by decree. This has energised his government - unfortunately, almost exclusively to do things that have nothing at all to do with the pandemic. First, his deputy briefly toyed with a plan to strip powers from city mayors, many of whom represent opposition parties. Then he threw a cloak of secrecy over one of Hungary's most expensive infrastructure projects, announcing a bill that would classify key information about a Chinese-funded railway for a decade. Next, he slashed bureaucratic obstacles to expedite a contentious construction project opposed by the opposition. Finally, he announced plans to scrap state recognition of gender transition. To give you some inkling as to why this man's position in the team is nailed on, there has even been a row about whether health care workers should be made to pay for their masks and visors. Classy. Hungary joined the EU in 2002. A core aim of EU supporters has always been to avoid the kind of totalitarianism that gave rise to the Second World War; paradoxically, Hungary now has a leader with very much the same powers as Adolf Hitler in 1933.

The middle order: four through seven. All English Test teams are fabled for a good middle order collapse. And, as a parting Brexit gesture, it appears that we have passed that collapse mentality onto the EU. Those who have lauded the EU project talked of a United Europe. Of standing together, of helping each other, of growing a better world. A bulwark against the superpowers; a line in the sand against another European war. What happens? A couple of bits of virus pop over on their holidays from China, and the whole sham is exposed for what it is. Zero cooperation across the EU. All countries drawing up their own nationalist drawbridges, and fighting in the dirt to get the biggest slice of the ventilator and PPE goodies. Germany and France standing aside so Italy had to go cap in hand to the Chinese to avoid having to float the bodies out to sea along the canals of Venice. The writing is on the wall for the EU; I can see them all falling like skittles before tea. I voted remain - I think I'm glad I lost!

Number eight is a key position for any team. After the middle order collapse you need someone solid. We're down into the bowlers, but we want a bowler who can bat - who can pull a rabbit out of the hat. So, who better than the good old United States of America? The USA - the most powerful country in the world. This has got to be a great selection, right? But wait. Do I detect a dip in form from our MVP, controller of the world's biggest economy, and the owner of more ways to annihilate people than any country on earth? Could the superpower mask be slipping? More than six and a half million Americans lost their jobs last week, bringing the total to sixteen million jobs gone in the past three weeks as the coronavirus pandemic has brought the US economy to a standstill. Sixteen million! Their healthcare system has been revealed to be only slightly better than that of Mogadishu, and their leader exposed as a gibbering moron, ridiculed at home and abroad. Yes, the mask is definitely slipping. I am now very worried about my number eight!

So, nine, ten and eleven. Who are the bowlers who are going to pull us out of the fire?

Well at nine, I reckoned the World Health Organisation was going to be our ace in the hole. If any organisation was going to ping down a few jaffas to ruffle up the virus' feathers it was always going to be the WHO. Except they have taken a real battering in the fixtures running up to this. Frankly, they've looked completely toothless. All talk. When push comes to shove, it seems they have pretty much no game at all.

At ten - and our last hope really - the Chinese. What's the world come to when you're relying on the takeaway wallahs to win you a game of cricket? But boy do they look sharp now! They bowled the virus out on home soil in short order, and they've been winning friends on tour all over the place ever since. On current form, they have to be everyone's favourite for player of the year. These guys are here to stay, and I think they might just win us the game. Though I'm not sure I entirely agree on their plan to put surveillance cameras into the dressing rooms. Well, the ladies' rooms maybe, but certainly not the chaps'.

And finally, at 11, I'm going for Jeremy Corbyn. Do I think he will make the slightest impact? No, of course not. He hasn't in the last forty years, why would he start now? It's a sympathy pick really. The poor old boy has spent his life trying to get us all to buy into his agenda for socialism, state-ownership and a massive public sector. Ten minutes after he jacks in his job as Leader of the Commies, or whatever he was called, the government suddenly has about eighty per cent of us on its payroll, and is imposing restrictions on freedom that would make Stalin blanche. It's all about timing really, Jeremy, but sadly it seems you are as rubbish at that as you are at getting the ball to swing. Or the voters for that matter.

11TH APRIL - HARD-HITTING INTERVIEW WITH PRESIDENT TRUMP FOR HELLO MAGAZINE

I meet up with the President in his beautifully appointed oval-shaped study in the White House. As ever, he looked trim and healthy, and even in the midst of this pandemic he made time to spend talking about the important things in life. But, as the most important and intelligent man in the world, he is a busy man, so I waste no time getting straight to the big questions.

ME:	*This is a very beautiful room, Mr. President. Tell me what you've done to make it so special.*

MR PRESIDENT: *Well it was bad when I first moved in here. Really bad. Really, really bad. That Obama guy had no idea. Those Democrats have no idea about design at all. No idea. It was all creams and pastels. Like their policies. Pretty much like their policies really.*

ME: *That's very funny Mr. President.*

MR PRESIDENT: *I know. I'm one of the funniest guys in the world. That Will Smith fella was only saying that to me last week. Said I should do stand-up and have my own show. That it would get the best ratings of all time. He said I was the funniest person he'd ever met. Even funnier than Christian Bale.*

ME: *But Christian Bale isn't very funny Mr. President.*

MR PRESIDENT: *I know that that, I know all of those comedians, they all really love me. Even the black ones.*

ME: *But, sorry, I interrupted. Tell me about your gorgeous office.*

MR PRESIDENT: *Well, as I said, is was terrible before I moved in. No style. They even had this great big wooden desk with loads of carving on it. It looked like it had been there for years. A real piece of crap. It even had a whole load of cigar burns in it. Anyhow, we got rid of that. We made a lot of changes. Great changes.*

ME:	*Tell us about what changes you made, Mr. President. Did you bring in an interior designer?*
MR PRESIDENT:	*What, one of those faggots. No, I did it myself. I designed all of it. I'm a beautiful designer. A great designer. If I hadn't been the best businessman in the world, I would have been a beautiful designer. Everyone tells me that. Coco Chanel told me that only last week. She was amazed at what a beautiful job I've done here.*
ME:	*But isn't Coco Chanel dead Mr. President?*
MR PRESIDENT:	*Fake news! That's just fake news. No-one dies here in America while I am President. Particularly since this Kung Fu Virus has been here. I passed a bill banning it only last month. The Senate. They tried to stop it, but they couldn't. I did that. I'm the first President ever to get a bill through banning death. It's a beautiful thing.*
ME:	*You've made marvelous use of gilt in the office Mr. President.*
MR PRESIDENT:	*It's not gilt. It's gold. I'm no cheapskate like that Obama dude. I spent over a billion dollars on that gold. Beautiful gold.*
ME:	*Wow, Mr. President. That is impressive. Did you pay for it yourself?*

MR PRESIDENT: *Well I'm rich enough. A billion is nothing to me. I've got a golf course in Scotland worth more than that. What a beautiful country. Apart from that Nicola Sturgeon chick. Although she thought I was a great. So powerful. She wanted me to grab her pussy; they all do. But I had no need to pay for the gold. I just cut back on spend on preparing for biological hazards. That was a billion right there. What a great businessman. I was so decisive. The Democrats, the House, they would have wasted that cash.*

ME: *You certainly are Mr. President. But tell me about that picture over there.*

MR PRESIDENT: *I painted that. I'm a great artist. Beautiful pictures. I paint beautiful pictures.*

ME: *Tell me about it Mr. President.*

MR PRESIDENT: *It's called Ventilators in the Morning Light. They all lied. Said we didn't have enough ventilators. The socialist media, the Deep State - fake news. I painted one myself. It's a wonderful painting. It will save thousands of lives. Then I'm going to send it over to my friend Boris. What great guy. Strong guy.*

ME: *I see you've removed the sofa where so many famous foreign leaders have sat and talked with other Presidents.*

MR PRESIDENT: *I had to. It wasn't made of gold, and still had stains on it from that pinko Clinton. He did an OK job for a democrat though; nailed a lot of pussy.*

ME: *And is that a work of modern art you've replaced it with Mr. President?*

MR PRESIDENT: *Hell no. That's a spray-tanning unit. Beautiful. Best spray tans in the world. I've got shares in the company, and we're starting manufacturing in the Ukraine next month. No tax and free premises. That's Zelenski for you, he really thinks I'm a great guy.*

ME: *So not because he wanted you to give him a whole load of military aid?*

MR PRESIDENT: *No. That's fake news. That Zelenski, he thinks I'm a great guy. Great tan. Beautiful tan.*

ME: *And its very avant-garde how you've built a three-foot wall down the middle of the office.*

MR PRESIDENT: *I said I would build a wall. Before I was elected President, by the biggest majority in history. I said I would build a wall, and that's what I did. I built a wall. A beautiful wall.*

ME: *And who paid for that Mr. President?*

MR PRESIDENT: *I said I would make the Mexicans pay for it. And that's what I did. And we haven't had a single migrant near that wall. Not one. Apart from the fella they sent to build it. Beautiful guy. Hispanic guy - really cheap. Those cartels, they're scared of that wall, that's why we've had no drugs in the US since I was made president with ninety-eight per cent of the vote. Not one.*

ME: *Just looking through the windows, Mr. President, what made you rip up the rose garden?*

MR PRESIDENT: *That was Mike Pence's idea. All those flowers reminded him of the gays. But it was my idea to install the putting green. It's a beautiful green. I'm a great putter. I had eighteen holes-in-one yesterday. Tiger Woods, he said I'm the best putter he's ever seen. A beautiful putter. He said he's glad he didn't have to face me in the Masters. And that's a guy who got a whole load of pussy. At least for a black fella from Wuhan.*

ME: *Thank you Mr. President. I won't take any more of your time up at this critical moment for our country.*

MR PRESIDENT: *That's good. I'm meeting up with Rudy Giuliani right after lunch. Beautiful guy. Brilliant guy.*

ME: *Will you be talking about the crisis?*

MR PRESIDENT: *Sure. It's a big crisis too. Serious. Rudi is starting to hook his drives, and we've got a fourball at Mar-e-Lago tomorrow against Rush Limbaugh and Jack Nicklaus. Rudi needs some coaching. I'm a great coach. That David Leadbetter, he couldn't believe the tips I gave him. Beautiful tips.*

ME: *Thank you for welcoming me into your home Mr. President. It's been an honour.*

MR PRESIDENT: *Yes, it has. A great honour for you. A beautiful honour.*

12TH APRIL - FOX ON THE RUN

I was talking to one my sons today, and he asked me why I write this diary every day. Why, when it is sunny, am I inside looking like I have toothache? I told him it was because I enjoyed writing. I like the challenge of finding something new to talk about, and the pleasure that comes from writing something I'm happy with. That there is a feeling of achievement in completing my missive each day - whether other people think it is good, or bad, or whether they are just supremely indifferent. That it's important to me to do something which makes me feel like an individual, with my own thoughts on what's going on in the world. 'Then why didn't you become a journalist?' he asked. 'Because, son, I'm not a moronic, braindead fucking lackey.' I replied, in that sensitive and restrained way a father should talk to his teenage son when asked a perfectly reasonable question.

Now, don't get me wrong, there are some excellent journalists out there. Men and women who search for truth, and can communicate with verve and incisiveness. These people are the not the common stock, however. For every Bernstein and Woodward, there is an army of talentless, valueless hacks. If you thought my mock interview with Donald Trump in any way amusing yesterday, I suspect, in large part, that was because my imitation of the *Hello!* sycophancy was all too recognisable. I'm not sure who reads *Hello!*, and I guess it is harmless in its own way - if publicly masturbating celebrities for their own delectation, whilst complementing them on the size and glory of their genitalia, is your idea of a harmless distraction. It's not my cup of tea, but hey, I voted for Tony Blair, so what do I know? But it gets a whole lot more sinister when journalists turn pimp, and uses their position to lie and deceive - to build a platform for their business or political paymasters. Fox in the USA has taken this to new levels. Josef Goebbels would have looked on admiringly, if the old boy had worked through his bit of trouble in the forties, and was around today. Here is some typically unbiased Fox commentary:

Doug Wead, for Fox Business, gave us, 'What he's doing right now, from the standpoint of history, is almost perfect. It looks like he was born for this moment.'

Sean Hannity managed to remove his nose long enough from the presidential backside to tell us that the Trump Administration's recent travel bans were, 'The single most consequential decision in history.' Nothing overboard there then.

Trish Regan labeled media coverage by other outlets as, 'Yet another attempt to impeach the president.' and went on to comment that, 'The chorus of hate being leveled at the president is nearing a crescendo as

Democrats blame him, and only him, for a virus that originated halfway around the world.'

Maybe these characters believe the nonsense they write. Maybe they think it is acceptable to lie and distort the truth in order to further their own agendas. Maybe they just get paid a lot to write whatever their boss thinks is a good idea. Either way, son, that's one really good reason I never wanted to become a journalist. But it's not the only one. I can almost take the journalist who is promoting an agenda; someone spinning whatever facts are before him into a web of deceit. In fairness, we all have an axe to grind at some stage - it is just a bit galling when we see the axe so obviously being honed on a sandstone of lies. But I like to think that normally I can see through this. What is, in some ways, more annoying, is the lazy, sensationalist journalism that tells us nothing, but is designed to provoke response. 'Click-bait', I think it is called in internet circles. If the good journalism is the thin smattering of snow on the top of the iceberg, and the kind of prostitute/propaganda journalism, so beloved of Fox, is the small bit of the iceberg we see above the surface, then this junk-food journalism is the bulk - the huge mass that resides below the surface. It's the regurgitation of information with no analysis, no challenge, no value. And, regrettably, this has been the standard outpouring from the journalistic community to this outbreak. Day after day we hear about the death count. Today, for some reason, ten thousand is a milestone number. Only if you're the ten thousandth person to die it is! If you're the ten thousand and first, then ten thousand and one is a much more significant number I will wager. Almost nowhere is there any analysis of the numbers and what they mean. Today about a hundred and twenty people died. There were less yesterday, but almost nowhere do journalists want to explore this. They tell us that the scientists say we can't be sure what this means. It's all about the headline; the ten thousandth death. Except it's not of course. The ten thousand are only the deaths recorded in hospitals, and take no account of (probably another twenty per cent) who don't make it into hospital. And there seems no challenge to the astonishing narrative - but one seemingly accepted at face value - that these numbers may actually not be quite correct because of the of the different ways that numbers are calculated. I mean, how hard can it be to count dead bodies? Nor do the numbers tell us anything meaningful about what proportion of the ten thousand may have been close to death anyhow - people for whom the virus was the final straw. In a normal month in the UK, forty thousand people will die anyhow, and a really interesting statistic would be by how much this had increased - not just how many people had Covid-19 written on their death certificate. Maybe it's us? Maybe journalists have long ago realised that we are so stupid, and have such small attention spans that only puerile headlines will garner attention. And, given this is a country which has given the world *I'm a celebrity, get me out of here*, and *Geordie shore*, I sort of get it. But a big part of me thinks it is lazy. Worse, it is a betrayal at this seminal moment in our history.

One of the shields the government has hidden behind repeatedly is how they are making decisions 'based on the science'. There is an inference here that science is factual, correct, resilient. In nineteen sixty-three. Sir Karl Popper published one of the seminal philosophical works of the twentieth century: *Conjectures and Refutation*. The book is a collection of lectures and papers that summarised Popper's thoughts on the philosophy of science. He suggested that all scientific theories are by nature conjectures and inherently fallible, and that refutation of old theory is the paramount process of scientific discovery. Should any new theory emerge as a result of these refutations, it would have a higher 'verisimilitude', and therefore, he concluded, be closer to truth. In other words, what Popper said was there is no 'right' science - just theories that were there to be disproved.

How does this relate to the situation in which we find ourselves today? Well, it is completely clear that scientists at home and abroad disagree massively about almost everything to do with this pandemic. In the space of just a few weeks the projections that different scientists have come up with for the spread of infection, for its associated mortality rates, and for the impact of different defense strategies, have differed quite dramatically. But where are the journalists investigating and trying to understand and weed through all of this? Where are the men and women with the wherewithal to dig, to think, to communicate? For the millions of people locked away in their homes, because the 'science' has dictated it, all they have been given are platitudes about 'supporting the NHS', and about 'saving lives'. Maybe this is right - but surely a governmental approach so besotted with science it embraced the 'herd immunity' theory - only to discard it when we realised that we didn't have enough ICU beds - might just warrant a journalist or two prepared to try to investigate rather than regurgitate.

Anyway, son, now you know why I didn't decide to be a journalist. But if there's a job going at *Hello!*, I'll be there - and only too keen to talk to Gwyneth about which shade of pastel vibrators give the best orgasms.

13TH APRIL - FIVE GO TO COVID COVE

'I say, Dick,' said Anne, as she eased her knickers back up over her knees, 'I don't know about you, but I'm jolly fed up with being stuck in the house. This isolation thing is just too bally much.'

'I know,' said Dick, distractedly, as he wiped his now flaccid member on Timmy's tail. 'There's just nothing fun to do anymore.'

'You could shag me for a change.' muttered George from the other side of the room. 'Even in a lockdown bonking your sister three times a day is a bit much.'

'Don't be silly George,' responded Dick gaily, 'You're about as attractive as Nicola Sturgeon. And besides, Ju and I always thought you were a bit of a lezzer.'

I'm dashed well not,' said George huffily, 'I've had more sausage than Kaiser Bill.' Dick and Anne laughed uproariously at this. George may have looked like she batted for the rug-munchers, but she was tremendously good fun.

'Woof!' said Timmy, wagging his tail. Unfortunately, this caused Julian to miss his vein with the syringe he was holding, and a small fountain of heroin squirted across the room. Timmy licked it up enthusiastically, and was soon lying on the carpet with a dazed look in his eyes. 'Drat!' said Julian, throwing his syringe across the room. 'I've jolly well had enough of all this. Do I care if the old people die? Not dashed likely. We've only got two weeks of the hols left, and I say let's go and have an adventure.'

'Gosh,' said Anne admiringly, feeling just a tinge of moisture starting to stir again. 'You really are a top bloke, Ju. I'm with you, let's get out of this flat and have a jolly adventure.'

Two hours later the Famous Five were packed and ready to go. Even Timmy was now awake, and licking the last of the cocaine of his paws. 'Shall I get the bikes?' said Anne.

'I thought you were the bike.' chorused George, Dick and Julian together.

'Woof!' barked Timmy.

To avoid the police roadblocks, they cycled by night, and during the day rested up in their tents, took copious amounts of MDMA and drank lashings of ginger beer. After three full days without sleep, and as dawn was approaching, they rounded the bend of the lovely hawthorn scented lane on which they had cycled the last three hours and saw the sea in front of them. As they heard the waves crashing onto the shore, Julian said, 'I am so glad we're here. I so hate the smell of that Hawthorne. It's just ghastly.'

'Did you know,' Dick butted in, 'that those dreadful French people think that Hawthorne smells of sex. I ask you!'

'Well thank heavens we saw sense and voted for Brexit.' opined Anne, wiping down her saddle with quite a large amount of tissue. 'The less dagos we have over here, the better this country will be.'

'Hurrah!' cheered the famous five, before sitting down to skin up a joint.

After they had all had a good toke, they threw the butts away for Timmy, and looked out to sea. By this time the afternoon was drawing in, and big black clouds were curling ominously on the horizon, exciting Timmy, who thought they were the *Pussycat Dolls* inviting him over for a pre-concert bone. 'Shall we look for a farmhouse, Dick?' said George.

'No George,' replied Dick sternly, 'it's lockdown. They will all have shut up, and gone down to the pub for a three-week bender.'

'Don't you call me a bender.' said George indignantly.

‘Don’t be silly old girl,’ laughed Dick, ‘we all know how much you like a bit of the old todger. But we won’t be able to find a farmhouse open with this pandemic on. And it looks like a rotten storm is on the way in.’

‘You’re right, Dick,’ said Julian, ‘the wind is getting up already, and I’m not sure the tents are up to job.’

‘Then what shall we do?’ said Anne, her lip quivering at the thought of a night without any nonsense. ‘Surely there must be somewhere we can shelter?’

Dick fished his map out of his rucksack, and studied it intently. ‘By Jove, I think I’ve got it.’ he declared finally. ‘If we just cycle another mile or so, then judging by the contours of the bay I am pretty sure we will find some caves to keep the worst of this beastly storm away. Though we might have to snuggle up a bit.’ he added, looking at Anne slyly.

‘You’re the best Dick.’ said Anne. Completely unsure as to whether she had got her punctuation right or wrong. ‘What’s the name of this bay?’

‘The name’s been smudged a bit by the creased page.’ said Dick. ‘Let me try and work it out’.

‘I can see it,’ said George, looking over his shoulder. ‘It’s called Covid Cove.’

So, as the storm rolled in over the cliffs, the Famous Five pedalled furiously towards Covid Cove.

‘I think I see an opening over there.’ piped up Julian, desperately looking for a place to dry his bag of weed, as the rain slanted into his face and the last rays of evening light disappeared, leaving a thick fog of gloom to settle over the coastline. 'Let's give it a look, chaps.'

Five minutes later they were inside, and five minutes after that Dick had magicked up a crackling fire out of some old shells and lichen. 'Gosh, Dick,' said Anne, 'you're just like Steve Irwin.'

'Just you wait till I show you my snake later.' chuckled Dick. 'And maybe George can have a go with Julian's little worm if she's very lucky.' And they all roared with laughter, as they settled down to BBQ the fish that Timmy had thoughtfully caught for everybody.

'Blah, blah, blah.' At first George thought she had been dreaming, so she settled down again. 'Blah, blah, blah.' This time a little louder. George slipped out of her sleeping bag, and moved behind the rock that covered most of the entrance to the cave. 'Blah, blah, beautiful, blah, blah, virus.' she heard, above the sound of a boat being pulled up onto the sand. She poked her head out from behind the rock. Two men were pulling the vessel to a safe position halfway up the beach. She was sure one of them had a familiar gait. And the other one looked oddly recognisable as well. 'Blah, blah, NHS, blah, blah.' she thought she made out. George rushed back to her pals and shook Dick and Julian awake.

'Not again, Anne old girl.' murmured Dick.

'Dick, Julian, wake up, it's me.' hissed George.

'Now George, how many times do I have to tell you,' said Dick, 'I will not do it with a dyke.'

‘Shush you idiot,’ hushed George, ‘there are people outside. I think they may be smugglers.’

At the mention of the word ‘smugglers’ Julian and Dick were out of bed in a shot - ever keen to expand their county-lines network. They snook out to the entrance of the cave, just as the clouds parted and the pale moon shed a translucent glow onto the beach.

‘This is so beautiful. So strong. I made it all myself. It’s all you will need. Blah, blah, blah.’ said the large, orange-faced man, holding out a small capsule to the other.

‘And it will be enough to create chaos?’ said his accomplice, staring at it in wonder.

‘Gosh, I know who that is.’ said Dick in an astonished voice. ‘Come on Ju, George, we’ve got to do something.’ and saying this he hurtled across the beach and rugby-tackled the orange fellow, while Julian and George wrestled the other chap to the ground.

‘Donald Trump?’ gasped Dick, as he wiped the fake tan from his hands.

‘Uncle Quentin?’ said Julian and George in astonishment, when they had pulled off the man’s fake wig and moustache. ‘Just what in the blazes are you doing with Donald Trump on this lonely beach at dead of night?’

‘I just wanted everyone to see how useless and overwhelmed the NHS is, and how we should contract-out healthcare privately to my company.’ said Uncle Quentin defiantly. ‘So Donald’s brought some more of the virus for me.’

‘Well, you’re going to jail for a very long time.’ said Anne, who had emerged from the cave in her cami-knickers and peek-boo bra to see what all the noise was about. ‘And you, Mr. Trump, are now only going to be re-elected with a considerably reduced majority.’

‘Hurrah!’ said the all of the Famous together.

‘Well I guess that’s the end of lockdown.’ said George, racking up a celebratory line.

14TH APRIL - GUESS WHO'S COMING TO DINNER

'And make surrre you put on zat tanning gel, Donny.' shouted Melania, standing at the foot of the beautiful stairway - a feature of the penthouse that spread over the top three floors of Trump Tower. 'I vant you look yourrr best today boby.'

Donald scowled into the mirror. 'Jeez Melania, don't I always look great. Hell. George Cloonie only rang me up yesterday to tell me I was beautiful. So beautiful.'

Melania raised her eyebrows to heaven, but resisted rising to the bait. 'Of kourrrse you do, honey. But today is rrreal special day. I just vant it to go vell.' She busied herself rearranging the table, and chatting to Stephanie, her chief of staff. 'It seems only yesterrrday when Barrron vas just boby. Now he has girrrlfrrriend.'

'What do you know about her?' asked Stephanie, who was getting slightly bored with this line on conversation. Making pizza and setting the table for her boss' little runt wasn't what she thought she would be doing when she signed up for this job.

'I hearrr she is verrry exotic. Like me I zink.' trilled Melania. 'Trumpy, boby, zey vill be hearrr soon. Hurrry up and put on yourrr korrrset and new vig I bought you. And get down hearrr now.'

Meanwhile, down at ground level on Fifth Avenue, a black limo drew up to the front of Trump Tower. 'Don't you worry, my lovely,' simpered Barron, 'they are gonna just love you. Love you as much as I do.'

'And I ruv you too, Ballon. But your fadder is such important man. I am velly nervous.'

'It's just gonna be peachy, babe. You're gonna love my mom. She had the best tits in the US before my old man got his hands on them.'

'Your fadder is voirent man Ballon?'

'Hell no. He's a pussycat. He wouldn't hurt a fly. And he's gonna be crazy about you. Come on, let's get going baby.'

As Barron and his new beau waited for the private elevator in Trump Tower reception, however, he felt decidedly more nervous than he was letting on. He was fourteen and in love, and nothing in the whole world was more important. What if his parents didn't like his girlfriend? What then? His dad was, after all the most powerful man on the planet. And, Barron knew only too well, he was a man who liked to control things. Barron loved this girl, but he loved the idea of that trust fund too - and of getting into Harvard without having to pass the exams. He took a deep breath, and pressed the button for the penthouse.

'Trumpy, zey arrre herrre. Be nice to zis girrrl. And don't grrrab poorrr girrrl's pussy.'

'OK honey. I'm gonna be great. So great. I'm gonna be so great, you're finally gonna let us have that three-way with Stormy.'

'I ave told you boby, I vill not hearrr zat tramp's name in zis ouse again. Now go open door.'

The most powerful man in the world did as he was bid. He opened the door to see his youngest son Barron, with quite the smallest creature he had ever set eyes on. 'Hey there, son. It's great to see you. So great. And it's so great you have a girl now. Not that I was thinking you were a bender - the Donald couldn't have a gayer as kid. Hell no. When I was your age I was doing my schoolin' at the playboy mansion. Hef, he used to say to me, 'Donald, I've never seen a boy the ladies love like you. You're a sex machine'. Such a sex machine.'

'Yeah, well Dad, this is my girlfriend, Corona.' interjected Barron hastily.

‘It velly roverry to meet you Mista Tlump.’

‘It certainly is Corona. Putin was only saying to me yesterday that how great it was to meet me. He loved my wall by the way. Great guy. Strong guy.’

Barron thought he had better take control of the situation before this turned into a press conference. ‘Come on in Corona, let’s go and meet mom.’

As they moved past the eleven-foot high gold statue of Donald, and past the several hundred pictures of him in the hallway, Melania threw open the door to the opulent living room. ‘Darrrlink, it is vonderrrful to see you’, she purrred. ‘But ver is yourrr lovely girrrlfrrriend?’ she added, looking around the room.

‘She’s here mom,’ said Barron, pointing down ‘this is Corona.’

‘But she so small. Is she midget? I zought I gave you lesson on eating girrrl. Stop at top of legs. Don’t eat all of legs.’

‘I am velly solly I so small, all my family small too. But I am velly kind girl, and I ruv Ballon velly much.’ said Corona.

Melania, turned and flounced out of the room. ‘Hell, take no notice of her,’ said Donald, ‘she only likes people who are beautiful. That why she fell for me of course. Took one look at me and grabbed my crotch. Said it reminded her of the Eiffel tower. That’s in Slovenia, you know. In Europe. I’ve been there. They’re renaming it Trump tower now. What a place. Great people.’

'You not tink I am beautiful Mr. Tlump?'

Of course you are honey, I love all women. They're all beautiful. That Nicola Sturgeon, maybe not so much. Or that retard Corbyn used to bone, hell, I wouldn't touch her with his dick. But the rest, beautiful; just beautiful. But, hey, let's go on through to lunch.'

All poor Melania had ever wanted was to marry David Beckham. But that bloody irritating posh bird got her tiny claws into him first, and now she was left with this fat orange pig. She had dreamt it would be all worthwhile in the end. That Barron would grow up just like Brooklyn Beckham - a vacuous waste of space who would date supermodels and wear the coolest shades in Vogue shoots. A proper celebrity. But what did she get? A ridiculously tall thirteen-year old who hadn't even twigged yet that his old man was a complete wanker. And now, to add to this, he rocks up with a girlfriend that looks like he stole her from a circus freak show. The paparazzi were going to have a field day. She'd told them all to be outside at four o'clock. Whatever happened she had to get rid of the kids before then.

When Donald, Barron and Corona got through to the dining room it was eerily quiet. It was obvious that, other than her chef, Melania had dismissed the rest of her twelve staff out of embarrassment at her son's diminutive girlfriend, and that they are just going to eat en famille.

'Seet down. Now, what vould you all like on yourrr pizza, as I av busy afternoon.'

'Ave I dun sum ting wong?' asked Corona, sensing the atmosphere.

'No dahlink. But You remind me of pet I had as child. I call him Tiny.'

‘Why you call him Tiny?’ asked Corona, walking through the open door.

‘Because he was my newt.’ cackled Melania nastily.

‘I think you velly hollible lady.’ said Corona, choking back tears. ‘My famiry very powerful in China. Evellyone know Vilus famiry in Wuhan.’

‘Vell, vi don’t you pack your tiny bag and go back to Vuhan. You not good enough for my boy. You not even got tits big as Kate Moss.’

‘I go nasty rady. But I no go back to Wuhan. I stay. I make you and your famiry pay.’ And, on that, she stormed out in tears.

And that, folks, was how Corona Virus came to stay to New York.

15TH APRIL - THE CASE OF THE MISSING PARTY

'Mrs. Hudson, there will very shortly be a knock at the door.' Holmes took his fob-watch from his waistcoat. 'If I am not much mistaken, in about four minutes. The man will be dressed in a shabby suit, and will have a straggly, ratty beard. He is clearly of a lower order, and shares little in common with Dr. Watson and myself. In spite of this you are to let him in, and bring him up to my study.'

'Why of course I will Mr. Holmes. I will, as sure as eggs is eggs.' And with this, Mrs. Hudson retreated, obsequiously, to busy herself with her duties.

'I say Holmes,' uttered Watson 'how on earth could you know all of that? With that extraordinary sense of hearing of yours did you detect a hansom cab at the top of Baker Street? And from the sound of the wheels, deduct it was a cheap foreign import from North Korea? But how do you know it is heading here? And how do you know so much of its passenger? God, Holmes, you do make me hot when you talk all detective like this.'

'Calm yourself Watson.' smiled Holmes, as he poured out two cups of Earl Grey. 'Some things are explicable; some are just my genius. Let's put this one to genius my friend.'

From two floors below, the sound of the bell ringing drifted up the stairs. Holmes glanced at his watch. 'Mmmh. A minute early. I am losing my touch. Still, let us see what this man has for us Watson. I will wager there is a mystery to be solved here.'

A minute later the visitor was shown into Holmes' study by an outraged Mrs. Hudson. 'Are you sure you want the likes of this vagrant in your room sir?' she spat out with some hostility. 'I can throw the scallywag straight down these stairs again. You just watch me, sir. I'll have the Peelers round here to give him a beating before you can say 'police brutality'.'

'No Mrs. Hudson, let him be. If my instincts are right this man has a problem to be solved worthy of the mind of the great Sherlock Holmes. Bring the man some bread and milk, he looks in need of a good meal.'

Holmes turned his attention to his visitor. 'And so, sir, how can Sherlock Holmes be of assistance to you this day?'

The visitor's beady, panic-stricken eyes darted between Holmes and Watson for what seemed like an interminable time. Eventually he spoke. 'Mr. Holmes...' Holmes raised his hand to stop him. 'Sir, from your accent I detect you have lived in London for some time. Probably north of the river I am thinking. Islington maybe? No, Finsbury Park. Yes, Finsbury Park it is. But you do not herald from this fair city of ours. You're a Wiltshire boy, I'll be bound.' And with this Holmes crossed his legs and took a deep puff of his pipe, all the while looking at his visitor. 'But I interrupt you sir. Pray, continue.'

Watson, could barely contain himself at this. This was pure detective porn. 'My word, Holmes, that is just incredible.' he interjected, adjusting the blanket over his knees to conceal his growing excitement from the visitor.

'Mr. Holmes, you are right of course. You have done your homework.' said the stranger. 'But firstly, I must apologise for being a couple of minutes late for our meeting, having promised when we spoke this morning that I would be here on the stroke of two o'clock.' Holmes had the grace to look rather sheepish at the visitor undermining his detecting powers, and avoided Watson's glance. This was probably just as well. There was nothing that got Watson hotter under the belt-line than the great detective at a vulnerable moment. 'Mr. Holmes, I come to you on an issue of great national importance. You are known as a man of genius. I believe you are the man who can help me get to the bottom of the greatest mystery of my life.'

Holmes leant forward. 'Go on sir, you have my attention. Is it a matter of murder? Or of a disappearance? Or of a great theft?'

'Mr. Holmes, sir, it is a matter of a great disappearance. Possibly the greatest disappearance of our age.'

'Is it the disappearance of a man or a woman, sir? Tell me such as you know.'

'Were it so simple Mr. Holmes. I am talking of the disappearance of over two million of our Good Lord's souls.'

On this bombshell, a silence filled the room. Then Watson began to laugh. 'Holmes, it would seem we have wasted our afternoon with this ruffian. The man is clearly deranged. Shall I have Mrs. Hudson show him out?'

Holmes set back in his chair, and relit his pipe. 'I take it Watson, that you do not recognise our visitor? Allow me to introduce you. Dr. Watson, meet Mr. Jeremy Corbyn. Former leader of the Labour party.'

When Corbyn had left, Watson and Holmes were left alone to think. As they lay naked on the chaise longue, Watson improvised a tourniquet on Holmes bulging appendage in order to find a vein into which to inject the heroin he so craved. 'My God, Holmes,' said Watson, 'it's good to feel clean again now that socialist scum is out of the house.'

'So it is Watson.' said Holmes licking his ear. 'So it is.'

'But what do you make of this preposterous theory he has, Holmes? That Corbyn lost the last election because of this virus that the Tories and the Jews developed. That they smothered it on the Chinese lefties who attended his political rallies, and that this infected two million people who were then unable to vote, or who lost their mind and voted for the conservatives?'

'It may seem incredible Watson. But just because it seems incredible does not make it untrue. Who, after all, would have thought it possible that Donald Trump could pass seventh grade, let alone become president of the United States of America? There is more to this than meets the eye. Of that I will be bound, Watson. I have heard talk of the existence of this virus - we must make its acquaintance. We must track it down and, when we do, then mark my words, no matter how improbable the facts that confront us, there will lie our truth. But that is for tomorrow, Watson. Tonight is for tonight. So, if you could just pass across the air-pressure vibrator so favoured by Ms. Paltrow, I do believe it my turn.'

Watson awoke the next morning with a hangover from the devil, and with a distinctly unpleasant soreness when he conducted his morning ablutions. When he waddled out of the bathroom, the mid-morning sun was streaming through the windows of 221b Baker Street. Mrs. Hudson appeared, and disapprovingly supplied him with a strong black coffee and one of her tampons to stem his bleeding. He could hear the unmistakable tones of Holmes' violin, so he made his way to the study. 'Good morning, Holmes. And how are you this morning?'

'Well, Watson, very well indeed. But is it still morning? I have been up for several hours already. Oh, and did I mention I had solved our little mystery?'

'Upon my word, Holmes, surely not. It was past two when we packed away the bondage gear. At what ungodly hour did you rise?'

'The early worm, Watson, the early worm. The time on the East Coast of America is five hours behind our own, so I reasoned that I might find people awake in the city that never sleeps. As you know, I myself spent some months there a few years back, so I am no stranger to its ways or to its people. It did not take me long to track her down to a tenement block in Queens.'

'But Holmes, what on earth are you talking about?' exclaimed Watson, all thought of his hangover now gone.

'Why the virus of course Watson. Corona Virus. An angry girl, yes, but she convinced me her anger was not directed in any way at the British Labour Party. No, I have a feeling the Republicans may be in for a hard time, but her vengeance is definitely not directed to this side of the pond.'

Holmes paused for some dramatic effect. 'So, I decided to dig deeper on Mr. Corbyn, my friend. To look closer to home.' If Holmes' first pause for dramatic effect was lengthy, this next one was interminable.

'Come on old fellow, cough it up.' said Watson, entranced, and strangely aroused again. 'What did you find?'

'We need to go back, Watson, back to 1979 when, if I'm not wrong, you were studying at Oxford. Well, not everyone was a clever as you, not everyone went to good Universities. And Jeremy Corbyn was one of the many, not the few. Jeremy attended the University of North London, but was sent down after a year.'

'I knew it.' spluttered Watson. 'The blackguard.'

'Well, Corbyn struggled to recover from the shame. Drink. Drugs. Eventually he sank to the very bottom - to left-wing politics. And, to prove his standing amongst his communist friends, to demonstrate his egalitarianism, he took to a relationship with a black woman. A rarity in those days. And it was not just her colour that marked her out, Watson. She was an attractive girl, educated with a fine degree from Cambridge. But one fateful morning Corbyn decided to show her off, and curry the admiration of his leftie friends. He took a group of them back to his house while she was still lying naked in his bed. Well, the poor woman was mortified and humiliated. She swore at that moment she would have her vengeance, that she would ruin and destroy him.'

'But how, Holmes?' interjected Watson, transfixed with this tale of love and deceit.

'This was a woman of guile and cunning, Watson. Had she chosen a life of crime, she would have had the brilliance or Moriarty. Of that I have no doubt. But she had something not even Moriarty possessed. She had dedication to a cause. And her cause was to destroy Jeremy Corbyn, and she sold her soul to that cause. She played the long game, A minor fall from which he might recover was never enough. She wanted complete humiliation. So, she stayed close, and, imperceptibly over time, changed. From a brilliant Cambridge graduate, bit by bit, year by year, she became - how can I put it - a moron. Everyone around Jeremy could see it, but so nuanced was her descent into imbecility, he didn't notice. Until, so extreme was her idiocy, that late last year over two million Labour supporters disappeared without trace rather than be associated with her. Corbyn was destroyed, and with it she had her victory. Watson, I can reveal to you that our culprit is not the virus. Our culprit is Diane Abbot; a true genius of our age.'

18TH APRIL - BRITAIN'S GOT VIRUS

The faintest hint of a smile crossed her face, those famous movie-star eyes betraying just a hint of amusement. Words were unnecessary, she had the attention of the room. Her eyes closed and opened again as though in slow motion, her lashes creating a breeze that stirred the papers on the table. 'No.' she said, simply. And smiled a little more. This was, after all, the woman who could put the cock into coquettish. This was Diane Abbot.

'What do you mean, 'No'?' gasped President Xi Jimpeng.

'Well, you remember when that Doctor asked you personally to take measures to shut down Wuhan, Xi?'

'No. Of course not.' replied Jimpeng haughtily.

'Then you get it, slope eyes. That's exactly what I mean by 'no'.'

'Fluck you bitch.' Xi was starting to lose it now.

'Noo lets tak' a momen tae calm doon a' body.' interposed Nicola. 'We're nae aff tae achieve anything lik' this.'

'Fluck you too. Nicora. I lun a cuntly with one birrion people. You take your orders flom fat Bolis.'

'Now, let's just hold on a minute here,' interjected Piers, 'we are more than half a page through this story and I haven't said anything yet. It's high time I did some virtue signaling in a loud and aggressive manner, whilst solving all of the world's problems without ever having to take responsibility for the crap that comes out of my mouth.'

Diane looked across seductively. It was the look that had first won the love and lust of that handsome young rabble-rouser of the left, Jeremy Corbyn, 'Piers.' she said demurely. 'Piers ...'

Just then a shadow crept over the table. In the midst of the argument no-one had heard the door open. As grey as its owner's t-shirt, the shadow's owner was instantly recognisable. For a moment there was a silence in the room. First to recover her composure was Diane. 'Simon, it's fantastic to see you.'

'Shut up Abbott you moron.' responded Simon. He was a man who had made his reputation by calling a spade a spade.

'Bit harsh, Simon.' muttered Piers.

'When I want you to talk, Morgan, I will write it on cue card.' levelled Simon. 'Now shut up, there's a good lackey.'

'Simon, is velly good see you.'

'And you Xi. And you, Now, tell me when is your country going to start repaying those loans I made to it?'

'Velly soon, Simon, Velly soon. Just few more nucrear leactors then we richest cuntly in world. Then we start pay.'

'And Nicola, how are you my darling? Stroked any Trump tower lately?'

'Whitevur the Donald said 'twas a complete lie. Ah ne'er gaed near his tower, 'n' ah certainly didnae ask him tae grab mah fud.' retorted an indignant Nicola Sturgeon, her voice high pitched, as a deep red blush moved slowly upwards from her scrawny neck to give some long-awaited colour to her pinched cheeks.

'Anyhow, enough,' said Simon sitting down and hitching his trouser waistband to nipple height, 'I didn't ask you onto the panel of my new show to listen to you bickering. Ant, Dec, get in here now. Explain to these idiots how this is going to work.'

'Hi Simon. An can Ah just syah yee are looking git tall an manly this evening.'

'I am, aren't I Dec. But stop being a sycophant. Ant, tell them the score.'

'Th' main aim o' th' shaw, o' coorse, is tae mak' simon even richer 'n' mair powerful than he is t'day. Noo, me 'n' Dec git ten million each fur t' series cos we oor national treaures 'n' everone loues us. Bit th' real genius o' Simon's idea is that each o yous pay five million tae be oan th' shaw. Sae he haes na cost at a'.'

'Ah think Ah understand what this English retard wi the sackless accent is saying, Simon, but why should wi pay yee when it's us deein the worrk?'

'Because, Nicola, being on one of my panels will make ridiculously popular with the incredibly gullible and stupid British public. And you four - with the exception of that orange imbecile in Washington - are the four least popular people I know'.

'Simon,' interjected Piers, 'you know that's nonsense. *Good Morning Britain* is the most popular show on TV, and I've been on *Britain's Got Talent* many times as you are well aware. I think you'll find the public loved me.'

'Piers. I will say this once. You're a wanker. You know it. I know it, The British public knows it. That camp tosser Walliams did better than you, and he's only got one joke. This is your last chance mate. Take it or leave it.'

'But I lun biggest cuntly in world. I no need for this.'

'Xi. I like you a lot. We've got a lot in common. But, if a certain tape of you pleasuring yourself to the Cheryl Cole logistics video were to surface ..... well, China can be an unforgiving place. Anyhow, Ant, carry on.'

'The show will be run ower six weeks. Each week wi will hev eight diseases performing, an wi will vote one thru te the gran final.'

'So, what are we looking for in these diseases? What is the basis for us voting for them?' fluttered Diane.

Simon smiled, patronisingly. 'You've not done this before, have you my love. Think of this as being like a Trade Union vote - you don't need to think, you just do what I tell you.'

'Bit Simon, ah ken a' body hates me. Bit ah haven't git five million poonds.'

'Trust me, after this, Nicola, you will have your independence. You will be the first queen of Scotland, and you will have all the money you want.'

Simon, you know alleady who win big prize?' enquired Li.

'Of course,' said Simon, 'what kind of fool would I be to have a show with a winner who I didn't know would make me oodles of cash?'

'So, who's it going to be this time? Susan Boils?' chuckled Piers.

'Well, the, smart money is on the little girl coming over from New York, mate. If I'm not much mistaken, she's definitely going to go viral.'

19TH APRIL - A WEEKEND AT CHEQUERS

I mean, talk about kicking a man when he's down! The poor sod is only out of intensive care for ten minutes and the vultures are circling. In fairness, it is a pretty chubby old carcass Boris has got, but couldn't they have at least left the lad alone for a few days until he got back on his pins. The papers today are full of the fact that he missed five COBRA meetings, and how awful it was that he took himself off for whole weekends in the country, rather than anticipating our impending Armageddon. Well I'm no Boris apologist, but it strikes me that he had put in a bit of a stint pre-Xmas with Brexit (if anyone vaguely remembers that), so he probably fancied putting his feet up - particularly after the entire country had been under water for a month, which seemed to take a bit of his attention as I recall. And to cap it all, he's just got his bird up the duff - and just ringing around his other offspring to tell them about their new sibling would take a fortnight just by itself.

Imagine you are at a COBRA meeting. I've not been to one, but I know a man who has (he revealed, mysteriously). Anyhow, imagine you had been at the pandemic meetings that our lazy, good-for-nothing PM missed whilst he was playing croquet at Chequers. One would imagine that, in addition to your good self, there would have been some fairly big hitters around the table. The Health Secretary for one, the Home Secretary for another - plus all manner of attendant experts. Now, I get having the main man being there might have been helpful, but what on earth did they do his absence? Did it not occur to any of them pick up the phone if they couldn't make a decision themselves? 'Hey, mate, hope you're having a cracking weekend. Yes, I know your busy racking up a big one, but it is important. It's that virus thing I mentioned at Annabel's the other night. Yeah, it turns out it could be a biggie. You're going to have to self-isolate and stay down there mate. No, it's not just you, everyone's got to stay at home. No, th medical bods are telling me we have to. No choice at all. Can we leave it a while before announcing? Why? Oh, OK, mate. We'll leave it an hour or so until after the totty gets there.'

Kier Starmer, who I confess I have taken a real dislike to already, is also a man on the anti-Boris bandwagon. Kier has been pontificating so much this last week, about how slow and useless Boris and the government have been, that I am genuinely concerned that the man will burst himself with his own pomposity. Kier, my friend, how do I say this to you? No-one wants to listen right now. Your time will come when we are through the worst of all of this, when people are looking for someone to blame. Right now, you just need to shut the fuck up. You're behaving like a teenager who's just seen his first pair of tits and can't resist showing off his erection to anyone who will look. Can anyone else imagine how great it would be to see Kier arrested in the early hours on Hampstead Heath, high on poppers and singing Young Guns quite loudly, while brandishing the kind of veiny vibrating device that would never make it onto our old friend Gwyneth's top ten list? Just on the off chance Kier should ever happen upon this page, and since I happen to know he is a lawyer, can I just say that I, personally, could not imagine this, and that I would fight any man who would in order to defend the honour of the man.

Anyhow, changing the subject, Prince Harry has been at his irritating best. Discussing the twenty five million pounds raised by Captain Tom Moore, Harry said how proud he was of what individuals across the UK have been doing, calling it 'the very best of human spirit'. He went on to say, 'It's also proving that I think things are better than we're led to believe through certain corners of the media. It can be very worrying when you're sitting there and the only information you are getting is from certain news channels, but if you're out and about or on the right platforms, you can really sense this human spirit coming to the forefront.' It may have escaped Harry's attention that not too many people are actually 'out and about' very much at all at the moment. The only people you can spot out are drug dealers and ladies of the night on their way down to Chequers. But if we ignore this oversight just for the moment, this is still quite astonishing chutzpa from a bloke who is five thousand miles away cosying up to Meghan's showbiz pals, having deserted his country and forfeited any rights to be 'proud' of any of us. I know nothing of Captain Tom Moore, other than what I have read, but I know he has medals from the same war my mum and dad fought in, and that he wears them to this day, saying, 'It's important. It shows that I was part of a very important and super army who were all battling for our country, which we're all so proud of.' Tom is probably far too much of a gentleman to say this to the Duke of Sussex, so I will presume to say it on his behalf. Harry, you are a person who was given everything in life, and yet all of this wasn't enough to make a man of you. Enjoy the beach house mate, just don't come back here any time soon.

21ST APRIL - HARRY AND MEGS

‘I say Megs, old girl,’ chirruped Harry excitedly as he walked out onto the deck, ‘I’ve just come across the strangest room. It’s got these really cold cupboards with stuff that looks like food in them, but none of it is on plates, so I’m not too damned sure.’

Meghan raised her eyes to heaven, and signed, ‘That’ll be da fridge yous uppa class cheesy pole.’

Harry looked at her blankly. ‘Er, what was that you said honeybunch? And why are you talking on that odd voice.’

'So yous iz sayin I've got da batty voice?' Retorted Meghan, defensively.

'Of course not. Heaven forbid my darling. But it's not, er, how one normally speaks.'

'Dat iz coz I as bin downtroddun by ya posh posse, an' made to abandon me roots. I natta in dis way coz I iz black, an' now I iz bak on me turf, I can natta as God intended me to natta - not resemblin sum over-privileged honkey ho.'

'Well OK, my little pumpkin. You know I will love you oodles however you speak. Maybe we could employ someone to translate for me, what?'

'Harry, iz yous frigin stupid. Yous nah we've no moolar now ya wrinkly batty Nan cut off our allowance, an' dat geeza who pretends he's ya old geeza hasn't give yous anytin' eeda.'

This went straight over Harry's head. Though, in fairness, that wasn't too unusual, even when people spoke normally to him. He thought he would venture back to safer ground. 'What-ho. So, what is that fridge jonny then Megs? Looks jolly good fun. And what is that strange looking room all about?'

'It's called da kitchun soft geeza. We all 'as one, evun hat da palace. Down those stairs ya Nan woz not lettin' let yous go down. It's where dey cooked dem sevun course breakfasts fe yous parasites.'

Harry still wasn't quite with the new lingo, but he had heard the word 'parasite' often enough to get the gist of this. 'Well, my gorgeousness, can I just say how jolly lovely you look today. Gosh, you're making me feel all frisky old girl. How about a bit of hanky-panky before luncheon?'

'Yous iz not puttin ya mingin honkey hands on me batty yous ginga dong pulla. Yous can't treat me like da slave on da plantashun, jus' der to be raped by da masta. Yous iz gonna get no 'anky-panky from I yous retard.' And, on that note, Meghan turned and flounced haughtily off into the house.

Harry looked after her, slightly bemused, and picked up his mobile. After finally working out how it worked, he connected with his brother. 'Wills old boy, how are you? How's Kate and the sprogs?'

'Tickety-boo.' answered Wills, though with an edge to his voice. 'Where are you? What do you want?'

'I'm somewhere in America, I think. There's a lot of chaps with bleached hair and surf boards hanging around. But Megs has started speaking really strangely. Honestly, I think I would understand that awful Nicola Sturgeon better than my lovely pookins right now. And we're staying in some sort of shed on the beach. Honestly, Wills, you wouldn't believe it. It's only got six bedrooms. No chance of sneaking any totty in a place this size.' he finished plaintively.

'Honestly, Harry, do grow up. One's made one's bed, so one has to lie in it. And everyone here is jolly upset with you, so you can't come home. Grandpapa said he would cut your balls off if he ever saw that ghastly tart of yours again, and apart from everything else we're in lockdown here. It's awful.'

'Lockdown?' queried Harry.

'Because of the pandemic, you half-wit.' snapped his brother.

'Pandemic?' said Harry. 'Wills... Wills.' But the line seemed to have mysteriously cut off at that moment, so he looked at his screen glumly.

'Harry, get yo ass in here.' came from inside the ten million dollar beach-house. With a deep sigh Harry pocketed his phone and went inside to find his wife.

'Does me batty chek massiv in dis dress?'

'Of course not my honey-cheeks.' gushed Harry, glad to be able to say something to please his wife.

'What iz yous sayin white boy, iz yous sayin I 'as got a mingin' scrawny booty? I iz da most famous blak actress in da world, an' yous tell me I ain't got no booty. I knew I shoulda boned wiv Jay-Z whun 'e acksed me.'

'I say, steady on old girl. We are married you know.'

'Married, yous brainless goolie sucka! I only married yous so I wud be more royalty dan Beyoncé, an' ya so fick yous evun managed to fok dat up. Yous told me everyone loved yous an' fought yous should be da main geeza, now some quillion year batty duffa called Tom Moore iz more popular dan yous fe walkin up an' down iz frigin gardun. Feck.'

There was nothing like Meghan getting angry to turn Harry on. He loved the way her eyes blazed, and her not-very-black-at-all cheeks would blush. He thought he would give it one more try. 'Come on Megs, how about a bit of jiggy time.'

'Harry, I iz not havin iuggy wiv yous eva again, until yous prove yous can do sumfink useful. Uva dan flyin dat stupid helicopta!'

Harry racked his brain. There must be something he had done that merited some nookie. 'Well, I've sorted out the virus.'

There was a long silence. 'You've done what Harry.' said Meghan. All trace of the jive from the hood now gone.

'I've sorted out the virus. You told me the virus was bad, so I sorted it out. Wasn't easy, but I put my mind to it and after a couple of hours - hey presto - no more virus problem.'

For all her faults Meghan was nobody's fool, and she swiftly calculated the popularity that would come with this fantastic discovery. In her mind's eye she could see the movie already, with her playing herself so brilliantly. And the Oscar, and the star on Hollywood Boulevard. 'Harrykins, come over to me baby.' she breathed huskily, her hand slowly sliding up the royal thigh....

Three minutes later Harry was lighting up his post-nonsense cigarette. 'That was bloody top, old girl.' he said happily.

'So, Harry, tell me all about how you solved the problem of the virus. I am so proud of my prince.' simpered Meghan.

'Well, first of all I twiddled on the knobs. And that didn't work. So then I changed the plug. And that didn't work either. Then I plugged it in - and bingo - worked like a top. Even got Elton singing mummy's song.' said Harry with a satisfied tone.

Meghan was not a little mystified at this response, and started to feel maybe she had counted her chickens just a little early. She looked over Harry's shoulder, to where *Candle in the Wind* was emanating from a radio on the table. 'Harry, I said virus, not wireless, you fucking moron.' she screamed, throwing off the bed covers and searching for Jay-Z's number on her mobile.

23RD APRIL - AND THE AWARD FOR …

It seems like forever since we were all locked up. And, whilst one of the mercies has been that we don't have to suffer endless interminable award ceremonies - where one lot of retarded half-wits gush about another bunch of retarded half-wits that they actually despise - this is proving to be less of a life-changing benefit than I had hoped. And so, my lovelies tonight, we present the *Wuhan Diaries Awards*. And the best of luck to all of you ….

We kick off the evening with *The Piers Morgan award for Most Repetition of a Misused Cliché*. This goes to….

'These are unprecedented times.'

Only a couple of months ago this was a seldom-used phrase, barely making ends meet serving drinks in a speakeasy on Cliché Street. But what a difference a pandemic makes. From obscurity it has been catapulted into the limelight as the stock 'go to' cliché to liven up really, really dull journalistic copy. You know the stuff. 'I am walking down Piccadilly and I can see only seventeen people and four cars … these are unprecedented times we are living in.' Now, I am the last person qualified to give a class in linguistics, but 'un-', I believe normally signals 'not'. And the dictionary definition of 'precedent' is 'an earlier event or action that is regarded as an example or guide'. So 'unprecedented' would seem to mean that there is nothing that has gone before that is anything like this. But, bizarrely, the 'these are unprecedented times' salvo, often comes in conjunction with some reference to the Spanish Flu pandemic of 1919. Which rather suggests that there is a precedent. Quite a big one, as it happens, as about fifty million people died back then of a virus. But hey, why worry about language and fact when there is fear and uncertainty to make really mundane journalism sound more exciting?

It's been a dull start to proceedings, but next up we have an award that will surely get the audience buzzing. It is *The Donald Trump award for Worst Human Being on the Planet*. So, without more ado, the winner is … cue dramatic drum-roll… At this point I would love to hear the gasps of astonishment at a winner who has come in from left field to bag the coveted award. Anything to liven up an award that everyone has known has been nailed on since the very early days of the pandemic. Yes, you've guessed, the winner of *The Donald Trump award for Worst Human*

Being on the Planet is… Donald Trump. Mr. President, congratulations on awarding this award to yourself. Do you have a few words for us before you present it to yourself?

'Hell sure I do. Beautiful words Great words. I've been reading this piece-of-shit diary for a long time now. I'm an expert on it. I know this diary better than the scum limey author knows it. You'd be astonished at how well I know this diary. But even though it's all lies and fake news, I am going to be bigger than that and present this award to myself. It's a beautiful award. A great award. For a great human being. Maybe the greatest.'

Mr. Trump leaves the stage to rapturous applause from the forty-three per cent of the American public who still believe he is doing a cracking job. As one they put down their weapons long enough to put their hands together for their exalted leader. It's an uplifting sight, made only slightly less uplifting by the thought that a good majority of them would be using those same hands to grab some unfortunate cousin's pussy later in the evening.

The third award to be presented is *The Margaret Thatcher award for Best League Table*. Our compere tells us that we are fortunate, indeed, to have the Iron Lady's son, Mark Thatcher, to make this award.

'It's Sir Mark Thatcher, actually.'

'Really? I am sorry.'

'Yes, really. Since 2003.'

'Wasn't 2003 the year your father died?'

'Yes, it was. But why has that the least relevance to the fact you should be obsequious to me, even though I only have an IQ of 98?'

'Well, I was just wondering whether the reason I have should call you 'Sir', Sir, is that you inherited your title because of the Thatcher baronetcy, rather than from your outstanding work profiting from arms sales in the 2004 Equatorial Guinea coup d'état? Anyhow, as you say, that's not relevant. Sir Mark, please open the envelope, and tell us who is the *Margaret Thatcher Best League Table of the Year*.'

'Of course. Before I do, old boy, you can confirm my fee has been transferred across to that numbered account in the Caymans? Yes? OK, and the winner is .... The Coronavirus Death Table.'

A young, Lesbian, Black, Jewish, Hermaphrodite-Arab MP stands up and walks to the stage to accept the award. The pressure of constantly feeling offended makes her look older than her seventeen years. She looks angrily at the audience, runs her hand through her short spiky hair, and starts to talk.

'This government is lying to us. We have been slow to understand, slow to react to Covid-19. Our leaders have failed us. At the end of the day, the league tables don't lie. The UK has the fifth most deaths in the world. There are one hundred and ninety-five countries in this world of ours, and we are in the bottom three per cent. Because of this I reject this award as a bauble of the capitalist state, and I urge to you all exercise your right to suffrage in the ways of our forefathers. Revolution, my friends; that is the answer to the question this virus is posing.'

She continued for some while in this vein, before exiting the stage to a smattering of boos. Even without her annoying speech, this had proved a controversial award. The most intellectually challenged of the attendant celebrities - all of them in truth - could see that any league table of deaths should probably take account of population sizes and density, as well as the propensity of a country to actually tell the truth. So, this was, frankly, a league table that was naïve, pointless and shite. There was probably not a person in the room who hadn't expected the Premier League table to win *Margaret Thatcher Best League Table of the Year*, for so convincingly demonstrating that Liverpool FC were, in fact, the best football team in the world.

After this, the final award of the night got off to a subdued start. But *The Diane Abbot Award for Most Blatant Interpretation and Exploitation of Events from a Racist Perspective* was always going to be keenly fought - by every minority group with axes to grind into their chosen racist oppressors' faces. In the end it was a non-event; the winner was incontestable. The programme for the evening included a quote from Lord Woolley, incredibly a director of something called *Operation Black Vote*.

'Anecdotally, we know that Covid-19 is having a devastating impact on BAME communities, particularly in England. We suspect that BAME individuals, including frontline and essential workers, are disproportionately exposed to this virus. If Public Health England has ethnic data on who's dying in hospital, they must release it. Only with transparency of data and quick action from all relevant agencies will we save lives.'

Quite righty, the government bowed to this cogently argued case, and agreed to conduct an 'inquiry' into why Black, African and Middle-Eastern people appear to be more affected by the virus. The audience rose as one to celebrate this achievement. To not only demand a government enquiry at tax payers' expense, but to do so in a way that looked to place blame for the vagaries of how this virus infects people, was a stroke of genius. How marvellous to make the case that black people were sacrificed because we didn't have the right data; that black people were somehow more brave because their odds were shorter - no matter that most NHS workers, black or white, and irrespective of the impact of the virus on their ethnicity, would step up to the mark simply because they are decent and caring people.

Lord Woolley of Woodford makes his way to the stage to collect his prize. I am presenting this award. I lift it up; it feels heavy in my hands. I can't seem to bring myself to give it to him. In the end I put it back on the table. 'Sorry,' I hear myself saying, 'it appears that we have an objection to this from every person in the country who doesn't define themselves by their colour or religion, so I'm afraid the award of this prize is going to an enquiry mate.'

25TH APRIL - THE A-Z OF A CORONAVIRUS WORLD.

A is for Antibodies. Basically, unless you've got a degree in cellular biology, nobody actually knows what antibodies are. But the general view seems to be that, if you've got some, that's an all in all good thing. And if you haven't, then that's a bit crap really and you're in for shitty time. It's a bit like having coke at a party. A is also for Andrew, Duke of York, who has so many antibodies they don't let him sweat apparently. A is also for alibi, which is handy Andy!

B is for Boris. As in 'Doing a Boris'. This is like throwing a sickie, just doing so at a really critical time so that you let everyone down. For instance, when Paul Pogba announces he can't play in the Cup Final against Liverpool because he's hurt his little finger, we will all say he's, 'Doing a Boris.' Actually, bad example. Manchester United will obviously never get to the cup final again. Silly me.

C is for Covid-19. Now, everyone that has kids or friends who work in IT will know that Covid-19 is a Star Wars character. A dark-side droid - R2D2 with a really nasty streak. Legend has it that Covid-19 was created by the evil leader Xi of the Wuhan galaxy, but this is unproven conjecture right now. One thing we do know - keep away from this boy, he can really stuff you up. Particularly if you are BAME apparently.

D is for Donald. Donald is a mythical character, with strange and disturbing qualities. First encountered by Ulysses, king of Ithaca, on his journey home after the fall of Troy, Donald had the unique ability to be just that bit worse than anything you thought possible - every time you see him. Which made him an alarming opponent. And first-class dickhead. He was rumoured to have been seen associating with the Simpsons some years back, but thankfully we have heard nothing of him since then. Could you imagine him being in a position of power while all this is going on? Phew, now there's a thought!

E is for Economy. This is another mythical concept. There is talk of an economy existing in our past, but no one is quite sure whether this was just a dream. In spite of this, some people in positions of authority seem very keen on it these days. They are forever trying to save it, or kick-start it, or fund it. E is also for Everton. Same things apply.

F is for front-line. This is anyone who is looking the enemy bravely in the face and saying, 'yah boo sucks.' to the little viral fuckers. These are the new heroes. Bankers, hedge-fund managers - you are the leaches hiding at the bottom of the pond, while our front-line attack dogs take all the risks. And when it is all over, you will feel terrible that you contributed so little, and you will have to make do with earning a thousand times more than those key workers. And just think how bad will that make you feel on the beach in Anguilla?

G is for Gwyneth. In dark times, finding a source of light is like scoring a gram of antibodies from your dealer. And Gwyneth is definitely my source of light - there is almost nothing she says that doesn't make me smile. Below are three of my favourites:

'When I pass a flowering zucchini plant in a garden, my heart skips a beat.'

'You come across online comments about yourself and about your friends, and it's a very dehumanizing thing. It's almost like how, in war, you go through this bloody, dehumanizing thing ... My hope is, as we get out of it, we'll reach the next level of conscience.'

'We're human beings and the sun is the sun - how can it be bad for you? I don't think anything that's natural can be bad for you.'

H is for Herd Immunity. There is lots of talk about herd immunity, and the basic concept is pretty simple. Most of us get the disease, then it buggers off as there's no-one left to infect. There's a bit of collateral damage with this strategy, about one per cent of the population will die. But at least we get on with life, and are not hanging around waiting for Santa Claus to deliver the vaccine next Xmas. This was the UK's early strategy, until politicians saw some very unpleasant scenes in Italian hospitals who couldn't cope with the overload. So we jumped ship, and went down the Santa Claus/send the world into recession route as it was clearly politically unacceptable to have half a million people die in full view of the media - who are keen to find someone to blame in such circumstances. As it happens, half a million people die every year anyhow, but at least they tend to do this away from the media spotlight, so it's not such a deal. Personally, I'm not sure where I stand on the whole thing: a bunch of stiffs now, or depression and unquantifiable human misery downline? I guess I'm like most of us - provided it's not my loved ones on the stiff pile, that herd immunity thing doesn't sound too bad really..

I is for ICU. These are very bad places to go indeed. My twins were in ICU when they were born. That was scary. How scary it must be when everyone treating you is dressed up like there's just been a nuclear spillage in the next room, I have no idea. I hope I - and you - don't get to find out.

J is for J.K. Rowling. J.K Rowling, in case you hadn't heard of her, wrote a whole series of books about a young boy at medical school fighting the pandemic. Check them out. Boris Potter and the Economy Falling Like a Stone. Boris Potter and the COBRA of Secrets. Boris Potter and the Prisoner of Azsuminfection. *Boris Potter and the Goblet of Antibodies. Boris Potter and the Order for Ventilators. Boris Potter and the Half-Blood Testing. Boris Potter and the Deathly Viruses*. Classics.

K is for Korea. Who would have thought - after all those years thinking they just made bits of plastic that kids could swallow and choke on - that it turns out these Koreans are the Coronavirus Kings. Test. Trace. Contain. Korea has around five per cent of the number of deaths of the UK, despite having only a twenty per cent smaller population. 'Who raffing now Tlump?'

L is for Lockdown. Lockdown is, apparently, the lake in Scotland where Denise Abbot and Jeremy Corbyn used to nip off and have a bit of left-wing nookie on a bed of red-hot Leninist pamphlets. L is also for lockjaw, which the unfortunate Ms. Abbot allegedly contracted whilst giving old Corbs a blowie on one such trip. Which, at least in part, explains the perennially pained look on his face.

M is for Meghan. At a time when the world is focused on survival, it is fitting, I feel, that her claim against the Mail on Sunday for publishing a letter to her father should commence in the High Court yesterday. Earlier in the week, presumably to position in our minds that the tabloids reporting on this trial as being vindictive towards them, Harry and Meghan sent a letter to the editors of the *Sun, Daily Mail, The Mirror* and *The Express* saying that, from now on, they would not respond to any inquiries from journalists working for these outlets. Instead there will be a policy of 'zero engagement', except when necessary through the couple's lawyers. I can't wait for her old man to rock up at the trial and give her both barrels - although it would be just her luck if the poor old boy got infected and popped his clogs. Here's hoping not, Tommy boy. I am so hoping this all ends very badly for the couple who have displaced the Beckhams at the top of the awful table.

N is for NHS. The NHS was born in 5th July 1948. On that day, doctors, nurses, pharmacists, opticians, dentists and hospitals came together for the first time as one giant UK-wide organisation. It was inaugurated when Nye Bevan, the health minister, visited Park hospital in Manchester. The newly created health boards took control of more than ninety per cent of Britain's three thousand hospitals, which had until then been run by charities or local authorities, but which were now nationalised. From the start, Bevan was determined the NHS should not simply act as a safety net for the poor, and that it be based on need, rather than ability to pay. Its first year's budget was four hundred and thirty-seven million pounds - about fifteen billion at today's prices, or only one eighth of our spend today. Nevertheless, financial problems ensued for the country as a consequence, and in 1951 Bevan, resigned from the cabinet when it voted to bring in charges for dental care, spectacles and prescriptions. In his resignation letter to Attlee he wrote: 'It is the beginning of the destruction of those social services in which Labour has taken a special pride and which were giving to Britain the moral leadership of the world.' It is fair to say that many people over the last month can trace the reason that they are alive today in a direct line back to Bevan's great dream all those years ago.

O is for Other things to talk about. Of which there seems very little right now. Bring back Brexit, that's what I say.

P is for Pandemic. I think we all know this one by now. It's like a 'potdemic', only bigger.

Q is for Questions in the House. These are those collections of words with a squiggly thing at the end, which self-important politicians shout loudly in the House of Commons as an alternative to streaking around the chamber naked and shouting, 'Look at me, look at me.' They are the cornerstone of our democracy.

R is for Retained immunity. I am jolly glad 'R' comes after 'A' and 'H' in the alphabet, or else this would be a really tricky one to explain. The sixty four thousand dollar question is whether, having had Covid-19, the antibodies generated by the body will provide defence against reinfection. There seems to be good news and bad news here. On the good side, it would seem that the half-life of typical antibodies is very long - which is why you only need to get injected once for mumps, for instance. People who either got or were vaccinated against Spanish Flu, for instance, are probably still resistant to getting it again. Although they would be knocking on a bit by now, so they've probably got bigger fish to fry. On the bad side, the problem is that cold and flu viruses mutate so rapidly that sometimes they're unrecognizable to the antibodies created by the body in response to any particular vaccine. And what we don't fully understand yet, apparently, is how this virus will mutate. It's a bit like teenagers as they start to grow up.

S is for Social distancing. This involves not touching, and staying quite a long way from other people. It's very similar to the rules the Jesuits used to impose when we had school discos as kids. Though I rather suspect they were concerned about a different kind of infection altogether.

T is for Testing. It seems that testing is the new sex. Everyone wants more of it, though not everyone seems to want the same thing. Personally, I much prefer the idea of the test that will tell you whether you've had Covid-19, rather than the one that tells you are riddled with the stuff right now. It's like having an ugly girlfriend - you'd much rather know it was in your past.

U is for Unprecedented. As in, 'Maintaining social distancing at a disco for hormonal fifteen-year olds would be unprecedented.' And not as in, 'These are unprecedented times.' You've probably got it. The former would, indeed, be unprecedented. The latter is not really true, is it? Strange; Worrying; Scary. But not really unprecedented.

V is for Vaccine. It will be a great joy if the Covid-19 vaccine is discovered by the University of Oxford project rather than one of the Big Pharma companies, who are all lining up in the hope of being the main dealer on the block. Donald is going for the low-cost option with his bleach injection solution, and I, for one, am rather hoping he puts it to the test by self-injecting during one of his daily briefings.

W is for WHO. You will probably have seen this on the telly of a Saturday evening. It's all about some doctor chap who lives in police box and travels around in time. It's a bit marmite really. The Chinese seem to love it - but The Donald bloody hates it, it would seem, and is threatening to cancel his subscription.

X is for Xi Jimpeng. Chief enforcer of the Chinese Empire, and father of Wuhan Skywalker. Will he redeem himself by saving world and his son? Will the Empire Strike back? Watch this space.

Y is for Yemen. They have just one confirmed case of Covid-19 - but he's as right as rain now and happily contributing his limbs to the civil war. I want to go there and sing happy songs. *We all live in a Yemen Submarine*, comes to mind.

Z is for Zero. The number of cases that The Donald predicted the US would have by now after it all died away in the April sunshine. It seems a long way from that outcome to telling people that injecting bleach might help combat the disease. Or maybe not. Just as bonkers.

27th APRIL - THE LOCKER-DOWN ROOM

The three of them had all joined the Zoom conference on time. They were just waiting for Steven Gerrard to join. 'I'll kick it off.' said Gary Neville. 'Gerrard is probably still 'unting round for that Premier League winners' medal.'

This drew a guffaw from Sir Alex, but a glare from Jamie Carragher. 'Listen yous. Just show sum respect to Stevie. The lad's a legend at Liverpoohl. One o' de grates.'

‘Yeah. That were dead gud when he slipped over and cost you the title.’ retorted Gary, stroking the bum fluff on his lip he liked to think of as a moustache. Though in fairness his missus rather liked the way it tickled down there on the odd occasion he was on the job. She had the joy that came both of not having to listen to him talk to her about football, as well as not having to look at his face. ‘But we need to get this show going. Sir Alex, Sir, I’ll start with a question to you. What do you fink about the lockdown?’

Sir Alex took a sip of his beer. ‘Ah think it’s nae pure tough enought, Gary. Ah bult‘ th’ world’s best team oan a stoatin’ defence. Ither than ye o’ coorse, Gary. Bit this isnae whit Steve Bruce wid hae dane. Whin ye hae a virus lik’ this ye hae tae defend deeper.’

‘Of course Sir Alex, yer spot on as always. That were a mint comment, Sir.’

‘Ere, Gary,’ interjected Carragher, ‘yer mike’s gowin to ger all clogged up wiv shite if it gets any ferder up Alex’s arse.’

‘Jamie. Ye’r richt son. Ah wish a’d hud ye playing fur us ower than that gobby wee fud, Neville. Mynd ye, ye did score mair goals fur us than him - even though ye wur playing fur th’ scouse jobby.’

Just at that moment Gerrard entered the room. Looking, as ever, immaculate, dressed as he was from head to toe in beige. ‘Arright lads. Sorry, I’m dead late. Me missus was shaggin’ some bouncer again, an’ I ‘ad to give ‘im a good kickun’. Yeah o’ corrrse. ‘Ave I missed anytin’?’

‘I were just askin’ wevver this lockdown was the right way to defend a virus with pace to burn, Stevie?’

'Yeah o' corse. Well yous 'ave to show a virus like dis a lorra respect. Wen I won de Champions League all my meself in two fousand an' five, Inter Milan were like a virus. Dey was all over us in the de first 'arf. Den we tracked 'em better and goron top, den we contained dem real gud after dat'.

Sir Alex snorted, and took a gulp of his red wine. 'Ay, ye wur awfy in th' furst hauf. Lik' th' chinese in Wuhan. Bit efter ye cam oot, as ye said, yer was oan tap o' them. 'N' that's whit we need tae de. Deny th' greasy fuckers th' space - proper social distancin'. Jus' leek ah gie tee that ither wee numpty, Wenger.'

Carra thrust out his jaw. 'I'm wid yous on dis one Alex. Lets 'ave a loook as dis on de screen.' He moved over to wall and started moving dots around frantically. 'Now dese yeller ones are de chinkeys. You can see dat dey are all far too close together in de midfield. Der set up four, tree, tree. Right? It's all wrong, all wrong. Right.' He moves some white counters into play. 'Dese white ones is de virus. Right. It's too easy f'rem. Too easy Gary. Loook as dis replay. Loook at de midfield. Two passes an' dave all been caught ball watchin'. An' 'dis is 'ow the games 'as gone on. De virus is settin' up chants afta chants.'

Gary is slightly nonplussed as to why Carra is suddenly talking about chanting, but Stevie interjects and helps him out. 'Yeah, of corrrse. An' it were only an 'arf chants when I scored dat crackin' 'eader to gerrus back to three one.' he said thoughtfully.

'Yeah, sound Stevie, sound.' a slight irritated Neville replied, in his most bored tone. 'That were dead mint, but maybe we can focus on the coronavirus.'

'Whin ah wis a' Aberdeen we lost a cup tie tae Coronavirus.' interjected Fergie. And after a large mouthful of his whiskey, added, 'Ah swore than I wid knock Liverpool aff thair perch, 'n' that's whit ah did.'

'Yous is just a fookin' alkie Alex. It were fookin' Cowdenbeath yous played, and yous 'ad never even 'eard of Liverphoool back den, yous Scotch dickhead.' replied Carra, thoughtfully.

'Yeah, o' corrrse.' said Stevie. 'I've gorra lorra respect for Cowdenbeath. Dey've got some top players. Top, top, top players.'

Gary could feel the conversation slipping away from him here, and with it his award for *Best Manchester-based-pundit-of-the-year* that he so coveted. He thought he would move them onto safer ground. 'Tell me, what does you all fink about the NHS?'

Fergie was first to reply. 'Ah think tis a pile o' pumpin' jobby.' he said furiously, spitting out some of the quadruple brandy he had had swigged back. 'That Phillip Green bloke is a robbing fud, 'n' ah wouldnt hae even paid a pun fur th' company.'

'Of fer fucks sake Fergee, warra yous been drinkin? Tellus, warra you been drinkin'? Dats BHS you're talkin' about, you bin'ead. The NHS is the 'ospitals. It's where yous should be. In a frickin mental ward.'

'Yeah, o' courrrse.' defused Stevie. 'I played in de NHS for a year. I've gorra lorra respect for de players der. Top, top players.'

No dey weren't Stevie,' remonstrated Carra, 'dey was a pile of shite. Yous only went der because yous got dropped by Liverphoool because yous kept on trippin' over de bleedin' ball. And besides, dat were de

MLS. Why don't yous understand? Why don't yous both understand? De NHS is de 'ospitals. Jordan 'enderson's just raised a pile of cash for 'dem. Dey're on de TV all the friggin' time lads.'

'But can we all agree that the NHS does some well sound work?' said Neville, sensing an argument building.

'Yeah, de do doh, don't dee doh.' replied Carragher, without a trace of irony.

'Well, on that note, I'd like to thank you all. It's been a well buzzin' chat.' concluded a relieved Neville.

'Yeah, o' courrrse.' concurred Stevie.

'Does a'body hae ony coke?' drooled Fergie.

29TH APRIL - WEDNESDAY NIGHT WITH JONATHAN ROSS

On the 29th April 2020 Jonathan Ross conducted an interview now infamous the world over. It is said that it has made him even more famous than Simon Cowell. It was the interview which laid bare the truth about Covid-19 to an astonished world. It was, as Ross himself was to say later, wearly gwate.

JR: *Good evening, and welcome to a vewy special Wednesday night with Jonathan Woss. Tonight, we have a world exclusive for you - the vewy first interview given by the most famous villain on the planet today. Put your hands together for .... Cowona Viwus. Cowona Viwus, it's great to have you on the show.*

CV: *I am very glad to be here, Jonathan. But why are you calling me Cowona? I am supposed to be a villain, you know, the least you could do is to pronounce my name correctly.*

JR: *Now, hold on just one minute, Cowona. Everyone knows I can't pwonounce the letter that comes after 'Q'. But you are the one who's voice is shocking evewyone, I think. Why are you not talking in a Chinese accent?*

CV: *Now then, Jonny old boy, you wouldn't be being just the teensiest bit racist would you? Just because I'm not six foot two doesn't make me Jackie Chan you know.*

JR: *But no-one else from Wuhan talks like you, surely?*

CV: *I wouldn't have the faintest idea, Jonathan. I've never been there. Never want to as it happens. Sounds like a ghastly place. Full of people eating dog-burgers and swigging rice wine - nigh on impossible to get a decent Chablis I would imagine.*

JR: *Now I'm wearly confused.*

CV: *Don't worry about it old chap. I do seem to have that ability with people. Scientists, politicians - all completely confused. I'm like an episode of Twin Peaks - but worse, you can't switch me off no matter how hard you try.*

JR: *But let me get this stwiaght.You didn't originate from China?*

CV: *Of course not. That was just a rumour put out by the Americans.*

JR: *Twump?*

CV: *Sorry, who?*

JR: *Twump. Donald Twump. The Pweseident.*

CV: *Oh, Trump! I do love the way you say things sweetie. It's just marvellous they've given you a job even though you talk like this. Really lovely. But no, not Trump - he's way too stupid to come up with that all by himself.*

JR: *So, who?*

CV: *Tom Cruise of course darling.*

JR: *Tom Cwoose?*

CV: *Of course.*

JR: *But why would Tom Cwoose want to tell everyone you came from China?*

CV: *Royalties and ambition, darling. Royalties and ambition. Tommy's on ten per cent, and he gets great tax breaks from the Chinese. He also wants to go places, and not just be an irritating little thespian with stack heels. Besides he thought it would be a bit of fun throwing the cat in amongst the pigeons.*

JR: *Tax bwakes?*

CV: *Of course, sweetie. He's got the whole thing sown up, Tommy's on ten per cent of the gross. Not even the net, sweetie, the gross. That boy knows how to cut a deal. Makes his Mission Impossible deal look lame in comparison.*

JR: *So, let's get a few things stwaight here. I can see our audience in the studio here are despewate to know. Firstly, where exactly ARE you fwom?*

CV: *Oh, Johnny, Johnny, Johnny. Where are any of us truly from? What does it mean to be from somewhere? Charlie Chaplin was born in South London you know. But his heart was in California. I always think of Charlie as a Hollywood boy, don't you?*

JR: *OK, then. Let's make it easier. Where were you born?*

CV: *Oh, I wasn't born old boy. Heaven forbid no! Not born. I prefer to think of myself as a creation.*

JR: *A cweation?*

CV: *You almost got that one old chap. Do you think they will still want you when you get the Rs working? I do hope so.Yes, I am a creation. I came into being and made the world a better place. Like a great painting by Renoir, or a sculpture by Rodin.*

JR: *Wenwar? Wodan? I don't understand.*

CV: *Well I only said those two for a bit of fun, Johnny dear. I don't expect you to understand.You just are a game show host, after all.*

JR: *Very dwoll. So, tell me, where were you cweated?*

CV: *In Birmingham, dear boy. Aston to be precise. But I prefer to think of myself as a citizen of the world. My offspring, as you know, are everywhere now.*

JR: *But how can you say that the world is a better place when people evewywhere are dying?*

CV: *We all die, Jonny boy, our bodies all die. It is not the 'if', but the 'when'. C'est la vie. Mon ami. C'est la vie. But the Thetan lives on, don't you know.*

JR: *The Thetan?*

CV: *Your soul old boy, your immortal spiritual being. My offspring are merely helping a small number of people to rid themselves of their body - although maybe slightly quicker than they had perhaps planned. It is a good thing. Survival is moving away from death and towards immortality. Surely you know this?*

JR: *Erm…*

CV: *Those who die come closer to immortality, Jonathan. Those who do not - well they get a few weeks away from the boss in lockdown, and save on wasting their grubby cash on a shitty holiday in Spain. It's a win-win really.*

JR: *You're losing me here. Let's get back to the beginning. You were cweated in Birmingham. Tell me more about this.*

CV: *It started with dear old Ozzy.*

JR: *Ozzy?*

CV: *Ozzy Osbourne of course. Lovely man; dreadful wife though.*

JR: *But what has Ozzy Osbourne got to do with this?*

CV: *Well, it was him who gave Tom the idea in the first place.*

JR: *The idea?*

CV *Yes, Tom was a big fan of At home with the Osbournes. Well, of Ozzy and the kids anyhow; he thought Sharon was an awful harridan. And he had heard a wonderful quote by Ozzy - 'Out of everything I've lost, I miss my mind the most.' Well this was right up Tom's street, so he asked Oz round to a bit of a shindig at his pad with some of his Scientology chums. Ozzy turns up, and hasn't been there five minutes when he's asking for a big line of Colombia's finest. Tom had to tell him that none of that stuff was allowed as it causes extremely damaging effects on a person-physically, mentally and spiritually, you know.*

JR: *I'll bet that went down well?*

CV: *Not at all well, I'm afraid. Ozzy was out on the deck when Tommy told him, and he grabbed a bat that was flying past, bit off its head, and told him he was, 'Guin ter snort the virus ert of thees fooker'. And that's when Tom and his friends had their brainwave.*

JR: *Their bwainwaive?*

CV: *Well they took the bat off Oz and gave a bit of marching powder to keep him quiet, And one of Tom's Scientology chums, who runs a big pharmaceutical company, took the bat down to his labs. And hey presto, a year later here I am. Me and my trillions of offspring, obviously.*

JR: *But why would the scientologists want to infect the world with a deadly viwus?*

CV: *Because they have the vaccine of course.*

JR: *There's a vaccine?*

CV: *Well you don't think they would let me out there without having a vaccine do you? It would be like letting Katie Price out without a muzzle.Yes, there's a vaccine. And when the death toll in America gets to half a million, in about July they reckon, the Scientologist chap who runs the pharmaceutical company is going to announce that they have it, and give all the credit to Cruise. At the same time, Tom will announce his candidacy for President. The Scientologists will sell the vaccine to the rest of the world, restore America's economic malaise and position in the world single-handedly, and Tom will walk into the White House next November.*

JR: *So, all of this has been a plot by Won L. Hubbards lads to take conwrol of the world?*

CV: *By Jove, you've got it.*

JR: *Yes, I think I have. I understand it all now.*

CV: *No, you've got it mate. Some of my nephews have just infected you. Have fun in intensive care, and see you soon old chap.*

2ND MAY - THE RETURN

Boris shuffled out of the door of Number 10. 'Fuck, look at his bloody hair.' said Grant Shapps.

'Oh, shut up Craps.' said Priti. 'You've not even got a bloody job right now. Who needs a Secretary for Transport when everyone's sitting at home watching bleeding Coronavirus Q&A on their tellies?'

'But really, he doesn't look great.' muttered Raab. 'He's always looked like a bit of a caricature of himself, but it looks like that expensive ventilator he was plugged into had a back-comb feature.'

'We are now beginning to turn the tide on the disease,' enthused Boris, 'there are real signs we are passing through the peak.'

'That's braw fur ye tae say, ye public schuil jerk, ye'v a'ready haed th' bloody thing noo.' said Alistair Jack to no-one in particular.

'Oh, do piss off back to Scotland - and give one to that ginger tart up in Edinburgh while you're there.' protested Alok Sharma. 'This is England. We don't need your kind down here.'

'Come on chaps,' said Rishi, 'we need to pull together around the PM right now. He's been jolly poorly'.

Priti Patel looked down her nose at Sunak. 'For God's sake you pathetic little man. Just because he plucked you out of your GCSE economics class and gave you a job doesn't mean you have to feel sorry for the idiot.'

Just then a piercing light broke through the clouds. Bathed in its glow came the woman with the longest title in British politics. *The Secretary of*

State for International Trade and President of the Board of Trade and Minister for Women and Equalities made her entrance. The rest of the cabinet were washed in her penumbra, and appeared smaller somehow. 'Hello Lizzie.' blushed Matt Hancock.

'My name is Elizabeth, as you well know, you complete waste of a cock.' glared Mrs. Truss. Her words were harsh, but her voice soft, her complexion perfect. The shafts of light glistened through her golden hair as though they were welcoming a new dawn. There was little that Elizabeth Truss could say that the male members of the cabinet wouldn't find entrancing.

'Yes, of course Elizabeth. I'm so sorry.' stumbled Matt his hand reaching protectively towards his now very diminutive member.

'I've heard enough.' she breathed. Even Thérèse Coffey was transfixed - thought it was hard to be sure through the milk-bottle spectacles and floppy fringe that had made her such a hit at the Ministry for Work and Pensions. 'It is time for Plan B.' And with that she turned, coquettishly tugged the hem of her skirt to her knees in order to arch her bottom towards the boys, and flounced out in the way she very much hoped Marylin Munroe would have done if playing her in *Liz Truss: the movie...*

Later the same day, the evening twilight was dimming, casting the shadows of the five people in the small House of Commons office against the plain white back wall. 'So, are you with me?' said Truss.

'Of course, Lizzie. Sorry, Elizabeth.' Spluttered Hancock nervously.

'I'm in.' said Raab, running his hand through his thinning, greasy hair.

'Me too.' said Gove nervously.

'I've waited for this moment all my life.' said Priti. 'But are you sure we can do it?'

Elizabeth drew back her shoulders, her perfect breasts seeming to hover weightlessly in mid-air. 'I am gypsy,' she declared, 'I know of these things. The old wise woman of the Truss clan has given me the elixir. Now we must go, the deed must be done before the bells toll twelve.'

Twenty minutes later the five conspirators had fought their way through almost no traffic at all on London's empty streets, and had nervously assembled outside the Old Burial Ground of the Royal Hospital Chelsea. 'Did you all bring what I asked of you?' asked Elizabeth. Her voice was confident, but her hand noticeably disappeared inside her skirt for as moment to stroke her lucky heather. 'Dominic, do you have the crowbar? And Hancock, the herbs and oils? Priti, the knife?'

They all nodded. The time for conversation was over. The gate was locked, so Elizabeth hitched up her skirted and shinned over the railing into the grounds. Any lingering doubt the three men might have had was extinguished by a glimpse of thigh at the top of her glistening stockings. The three of them were up and over in the blink of an eye. Priti raised her eyes to heaven. 'Men!' she muttered, as she followed them over the fence.

It didn't take them long to find the spot. Elizabeth Truss looked at it reverently. 'OK Dominic, get the stone up.' Rabb got to work, and in five minutes the flat stone had been set aside, leaving a small compartment in which stood a royal blue and gold casket. Elizabeth reached in took it out, turning it in her hands, and with a far-away look in her eyes. 'Hancock, mix up the oils and herbs.' She slowly unscrewed the top of the casket. 'Ok, pour it in'. Hancock did as bid.

'What would you like me to do?' enquired Gove, nervously.

'Oh Michael, but you're the most important person here.' intoned Elizabeth. 'Priti...'

And with that Priti stepped in front of Gove, and put her hand to his cheek. Gove's astonishment was profound. He had never before seen Priti Patel show affection to another human being. He was still contemplating this thought when her hand moved round to the back of his head, grabbed his hair, and yanked his head back. In a single movement she drew her knife across his throat, and Gove's blood spurted high into the night air as he gargled away his last moments on this earth. Elizabeth positioned the casket so several drops entered and mingled with the ashes and gypsy herbal potion. For a few moments nothing happened. Time seemed to stand still. Then smoke began to pour from the casket, a little to begin with, then a burgeoning cloud. The smoke didn't dissipate, but slowly formed into a shape. Unrecognisable at first, then eerily familiar. The four remaining conspirators looked on transfixed, until an enormous clap of thunder startled them to look upwards and see a fork of lightening rushing through the air to strike the ground at the very centre of the smoke cloud. It was too much for Hancock, who lost control of his bladder, and a steady stream of urine puddled into the cavity which only moments earlier had housed the urn.

'The problem with pissing in my grave is that you will eventually run out of piss.' smirked the woman, dressed from head to toe in blue, that now stood before them. 'But it's good to see I can still make you morons wet yourselves.' Margaret Thatcher was back.

...To be continued...

3RD MAY - THE RETURN. PART II

Thatcher sat at the head of the table of the Briefing Room, a look of wonder on her face. 'So, you had several weeks to make decisions and didn't make then. Is that the long and short of this then?'

Boris shifted uncomfortably in his chair. 'Ermm.'

'Well is it or isn't it, you cretin?' snapped the Iron Lady.

'Are you sure no-one saw you coming in the building?' said Boris, desperately trying to change the subject.

'They'll know I'm back soon enough. Tell me, is this a new thing?'

'What?' asked Boris.

That nobody answers a direct fucking question you ridiculous Wersel Gummidge lookalike?' thundered Thatcher.

'Ah. Well. I guess we could have made some decisions a tiny bit quicker.' muttered, Boris, avoiding the Iron Lady's piercing glare.

'Three days!'

'Pardon?'

'What did you do in the first three days after this virus first arrived in the UK?' She looked at her notes, 'On the twenty-eighth of February I believe.'

Boris consulted his diary. 'That was a Friday. Mmmh, pretty sure I had some chums down at Chequers that weekend. But I was back by Monday lunchtime. Definitely. Matt popped over and we had a bit of a chat about it Monday afternoon. Isn't that right Matt?'

Hancock nodded, and squirmed uncomfortably in his chair. He hadn't had the opportunity yet to change his trousers after his unfortunate accident earlier in the evening, and his trousers were decidedly squelchy.

'Do you know what I did in the three days after The Argies invaded the Falklands?' queried Thatcher. 'Which was also a Friday as it happens.'

Boris twiddled his hair, doing an excellent impression of a first former in the headmaster's office after he'd been caught smoking in the school toilets. 'Not really.' he replied.

'I put together a task force to sail over to the South Atlantic and kick their wop arses.' shouted Thatcher, banging the desk loudly, and causing Hancock to emit the final bit of pee left in his overwrought bladder. 'That's what I did, you pathetic excuse for a man. Whilst you were down at Chequers, with your posh mates, seeing who could jerk off the fastest. And do you know what we did seven weeks after that?'

The Prime Minster was not liking this grilling at all. He was starting to pine for happier days in intensive care - particularly with that New Zealand nurse with the nice knockers who has been so lovely to him.

'We accepted their unconditional surrender.' Thatcher sat back in her chair and surveyed the room around her. Where was the Heseltine? The Keith Joseph? Where was the Jon Nott, or the Wille Whitelaw? Her steely blue eyes looked from Boris to Hancock to Raab, and she shook her head dolefully. The only two men in the room worthy of the name were Priti Patel and Liz Trust.

'And what happened here seven weeks later,' she consulted her dairy, 'on the seventeenth of April 2020?'

Matt shuffled the papers on his desk and avoided her gaze. He was conscious too that he was starting to whiff a little, and was desperately hoping that Margaret would not detect this and spot another weakness.

'I'll tell you, shall I? Seven hundred and thirty-eight people died in hospitals - and probably hundreds more in Care Homes, that you were too bloody incompetent to count. Seven hundred and thirty-eight! That's almost exactly three times the number of our brave troops who died in the whole of the Falklands War.'

Raab started to mumble something about this being a different kind of war, but was silenced by the Iron Lady's glare. 'OK, I will accept that it was a complicated situation way, beyond the limited ability of idiots like you, but presumably at least we were prepared for the fight when it got here. I imagine we had plenty of PPE to protect our doctors and nurses?'

Hancock could feel that he was very close to adding some poo to the pee washing around in his pants. 'We've been scouring the world for the very best PPE available.' he asserted. 'We've got so much that sometimes our nurses don't even have to take it home and pop it in their washing machines of an evening.' he added, not altogether convincingly.

'So, we didn't have stockpiles then?' she asked, looking genuinely astonished.

'Yes, of course we did.' interjected Boris. 'Well, maybe not quite enough. Well, actually I suppose we were caught a little bit on the hop.'

'Nine months.' said Thatcher sternly.

'Nine months. Yes, exactly. Carrie popped little Wilfred out right on the dot of nine months.' said Boris brightly, glad to move on to a happier subject.

'I'm not talking about your ghastly little sprog, Johnson. Nine months' supply was the amount of coal I had had stockpiled so I could defeat the miners and rid us of scourge of Trade Union power.' For a moment Margaret allowed herself the indulgence of recalling those happy days. Glorious images of pit closures, and police charging striking miners with their batons drawn, floated across her mind. Little did people know all those years ago that she was the first great environmental warrior. Today she would be a darling of the left for ridding the world of fossil fuels, rather than its comic-book villain. Greta Thunberg would call her Aunty Margaret, and Arthur Scargill would be about as popular as Richard Branson had just become. She pulled herself back from her reverie. 'And what of our EU partners? I suppose we are paying for all of their bloody PPE as usual? While the bloody French swig wine and turn up their noses at us?'

'We're not in the EU any more Mrs. Thatcher.' said Boris, in the manner of a teenager telling his mum he was gay, and not being quite sure how she would take it.

'We're not in the EU?' whispered Mrs Thatcher, so softly almost no-one could make out what she said.

'No.' stuttered Boris. 'I concluded the deal to take us out just before Christmas'.

Margaret stood up and slowly walked around the table. She sniffed a little as she passed Hancock, but didn't allow the rather unpleasant smell emanating from him to distract her. She stood in front of Boris, and looked down at him. Her expression was impossible to fathom, and the tension in the air was palpable. After what seemed an eternity, a smile spread across her face, and the Iron Lady slid sexily onto his lap and looked hungrily into his eyes. 'I think maybe I've got you all wrong,

Boris. It seems like you're doing a pretty great job after all.' she purred. 'Maybe we could talk privately?' she said, for the benefit of the others, and then putting he mouth close to his ear so they couldn't hear, she whispered, 'I think its blo-jo time for Bojo. Don't you my darling?'

6TH MAY - THE RETURN. PART III

Margaret sat in the shadows at the back of the room. Liz Truss sat beside her, and it was fair to say that Liz was less than happy with the situation. Not with Margaret being in the shadows - after all she had never wanted Margaret to take the limelight from her. But in her mind's eye she had seen Margaret as coming back, kicking ass - particularly fat ventilator-boy's ass - before ordaining the lovely Ms. Truss as her natural successor, and returning to the fires of hell to once again make Lucifer's life a bloody misery. The wise woman of her clan had assured her that the potion to bring Mrs. Thatcher back to life would only work for twenty-four hours. But Liz, not for the first time, was an MP feeling who was starting to think that the whole EU thing may well have truly fucked her plans.

Margaret, in a different, and altogether less metaphorical way, was feeling well and truly fucked as well. The quick blowie she had planned to give to Boris as reward for Brexit had led to an altogether more passionate evening. She had never had a fatty before, but it turned out she couldn't get enough of it. Dennis was a lovely bloke, of course he was; the love of her life. But, frankly, he did have a bit of a scrawny butt - where Bojo's was bountiful beyond her dreams. If the Dennis Thatcher arse was one of the smaller Orkney Islands: small, craggy, and needing more exposure to sunshine - the Boris arse was Greenland: huge, soft to the touch, and surprisingly warm under that fur blanket. Margaret was unaccustomed to wasting time contemplating issues of a more personal nature, not when there were Unions to be broken and wops to be put in their place, but, and perhaps for the first time in her life, her girly heart was fluttering. Lustful thoughts were supplanting the thinking of John Maynard Keynes at the forefront of that brilliant mind. A never-before-seen blush crept up her face as she recalled the intimacies of that first evening: the first kiss, the meaningful glances, the moment when Boris had casually cast aside those enormous boxers to reveal himself in all his glory to the former Premier. Maybe she wasn't too old to have another baby? A boy, maybe? It would be different this time. Not like that limp-wristed excuse she had sired first time round. No, this would be a proper man. A man the press would love; they would call him the Iron Sausage. He would be the man to finally destroy the Labour Party, and ensure that free milk for schoolkids was made illegal the whole world over.

Whilst Margaret was happily allowing her attention to wander from proceedings in the room, Elisabeth was equally distracted, trying to figure out what had gone wrong. Three days had gone by and Thatcher was still very much alive. Rather than disappearing in a cloud of smoke when the bells tolled midnight, as she had been promised by the wise woman, she was very much still here. And with an odd faraway look in her eyes that was most disconcerting. At first, she had thought that maybe the herbs in the potion had been too strong, but Hancock had told her that he had bought them in Aldi when he was out shopping for coveralls for the NHS, so this didn't seem likely. Then she had thought that maybe she had used too much of Gove's blood, but when she recalled how insipid and watery it has looked as it had dribbled down her arm, this didn't seem likely either. Frankly, Gove hadn't looked like he had enough red blood cells to fuel an erection in a humming bird. No, something had gone very wrong to overturn the gypsy charm that had brought Margaret Thatcher back from the grave, and she needed to find out what.

Boris finished speaking, and looked around the room. It was a meeting of his inner cabinet, and they had always been a rebellious, moody bunch. He had only got Brexit through by threating to invite the Labour Party and the Muslim Anarchists to a government of national unity, and his ministers had all been spoiling for a fight ever since. But now, amazingly, they were in total agreement with everything he proposed. He had the distinct view that, if he had suggested continuing the lockdown with Diane Abbot moving in with each of them in turn, they would have happily agreed. Something had changed. He glanced to the far end of the room at Mrs. Thatcher, who returned his glance with a kittenish smile, and the first glimmer of an understanding dimly crossed his mind.

'We need to talk.' said a tight-lipped Liz Truss, as Boris made his way out of the room.

'Maybe later babes.' said Boris, even now not completely out of reach of Elizabeth's considerable charms.

'Now.' barked Truss. 'Without her.' she added, gesturing at Thatcher.

Boris and Liz retired to a small ante-room, though not before Margaret passed him a small folded note. Boris opened it to reveal a rather cleverly drawn picture of Michael Foot performing a sex act on Josef Stalin, set above a love heart with 'Boris & Mags' engraved inside it. He ran his tongue lasciviously over his lips, and smiled at her before he closed the door.

'Something is very wrong Boris.' whispered Truss. 'I admit, I got her here to try and wrench power from you, and that's not worked. But I can live with that. But why is she still here? She's creeping me out. I've talked to the wise woman, and no-one has ever been brought back for more than twenty-four hours. She tells me something terrible will happen unless she returns to the spirit world.'

'But I'm liking her being around Liz. She's really helping me. I feel stronger with her around. And everyone does what I tell them. It's bloody great - it's what I thought being PM would be like.' enthused Boris. 'And besides, she's pretty hot in the old sack as well.'

Liz chose to ignore this last rather unwelcome piece of information. 'She's coating you, Boris.'

'What do you mean she's 'coating' me?'

'The old woman told me what happens when people come back. Fragments of their soul, quite literally, rub off on you. You acquire bits their character, bits of their personality.' Boris looked at her uncomprehendingly. Liz put it on terms he might understand, 'It's like a virus, Boris, it takes you over. Normally when people come back, they die again in a day, so you recover. But the old woman says that if it goes on longer, if she lives longer, your defenses will be overwhelmed.' Boris was clearly still struggling to come to terms with this, so Liz laid it on the line, 'Boris, if this goes on to the end of the week you will have beautifully coiffed hair, a perfectly pressed blue suit, and you'll be jerking off to pictures of Ronald Reagan. Think on my friend.'

Margaret had been left by herself for the first time since her rebirth, and her mind started to turn. Yes, she felt these strange emotions. But it was more than just young love, she knew that. She could feel herself drifting, as though she wasn't quite of this world. But then she and Boris would make sweet love, and she would feel whole again. She would be the Iron Lady. But then, gradually, she would feel herself fading. Until Boris, lovely Boris, ravished her once more. There was a cycle, she could see that, and she was determined to get to the bottom of it. That lovely Greenland of a bottom.

The call came into the house in LA later that evening. Gwyneth Paltrow switched off her vibrator and floated across the floor to answer it. 'Liz Truss here.' breathed a voice at the other end.

'Who?'

'Liz Truss, UK Secretary of State for International Trade and President of the Board of Trade and Minister for Women and Equalities.'

'Gosh, what a big title. I had less words to say in my last movie.' giggled Gwyneth enviously. 'But what can I do for you Fizz, sweetie?'

'Liz.' snarled Liz, already irritated by this woman. 'There's some fucking weird stuff going on over here, and you're the weirdest person I've ever heard of, so you just might be useful. So, what you can do, sweetie, unless you want HMRC on your back for the next five years, is get on a flight over here. Right now.'

Twenty-four hours later Truss, Hancock and Paltrow were secreted away in a safe room far from prying eyes. 'So, that's how she got back, and now she just won't bloody die again.' concluded Liz.

'And you say she is having regular sex with Boris?' questioned Gwyneth.

'Can't prise the bloody two of them apart.' said Hancock ruefully, in the tone of a man for whom very little prising had ever been called for.

'Isn't it obvious?' asked Gwyneth.

'Clearly not, or we wouldn't have sent a private plane to get your bony ass over here.' said Liz, who was even less taken by Ms. Paltrow in the flesh than she was over the phone.

'Well, if you read my article on Goop it would be!' And in response to Matt's blank look, 'That's my wellness and lifestyle website, sweetie.' Matt had no lifestyle, and had only recently heard of wellness as so many people seemed to be not very well at all, so this didn't fully clear things up for him at all.

‘Just tell us please, Gwyneth.’ huffed Liz through gritted teeth.

‘Semencronology.’ asserted Gwyneth, and took a sip of her koala-bear-urine tea as she sat back in her chair feeling pleased with herself.

‘Semencronology?’ asked Liz, not too keen on where she thought this conversation might be heading.

‘Yes. Some men have unusually powerful semen, which can breathe life into women. Usually they are actors and rock stars of course, but occasionally one finds an ordinary man with this quality. It’s very rare though. It’s why Goop moisturizer is so expensive, it’s so hard to get the supply.’

Liz felt slightly faint at this, as she had sampled some of Ms. Paltrow’s products in the past. She pulled herself together, ‘So, what your telling me is that it’s Boris’ jizz that’s keeping the old bat alive?’ she mused thoughtfully, the outline of a plan forming.

An hour later Truss and Hancock were travelling back into London in Matt’s Vauxhall Nova. ‘I can’t do it Liz. It’s immoral. First killing Gove, then this. When will it stop?’

‘When it’s over Matt, when it’s over. Do you want her around in the background for the whole of this parliament? You’d be wetting yourself every day - you couldn’t afford the dry-cleaning bills.’

An hour after that they were in Number 10, sitting opposite an astonished Boris Johnson. ‘So, what you’re telling me is that they found out, from all the tests and samples they took from me when I was in intensive care, that I have the vaccine? And that I’m the only one who has it?’

'Yep,' said Truss, as Hancock shifted uneasily in his seat, 'just you, Boris. Isn't it amazing?'

'And this vaccine is in my semen?' He thought for a moment, 'But why did they take a sample of my semen?'

'Well that New Zealand nurse,' said Liz, 'she was very pretty .....'

'Yes, yes.' said Boris hurriedly. 'So, what do we do now?'

'Well,' said Hancock, 'I've spoken to Whitty, the CMO, and he says we have to get all the supply from you that we can. We only need a tiny bit for each person - in three weeks we will have inoculated the whole country.'

Boris drew back his shoulders, and gazed beyond Truss and Hancock to a future where he was no longer the clown, but the saviour of the world. He liked what he saw.

'Of course,' said Liz, interjecting into his Churchillian fantasy, 'you will have to stop boning Margaret - there would be hell to play if the public found out you are wasting any.'

'Fair enough.' said Boris. 'If I'm honest I getting a bit bored anyhow. The bloody woman is so needy, and keeps on trying to brush my hair. Besides, Carrie is getting a bit suspicious as I haven't been to see the baby yet.' He looked at Hancock, 'Matt, give the order to lift the lockdown. Send everyone back to work'.

And that, readers, is the incredible story of how the second wave started.

8TH MAY - VE DAY

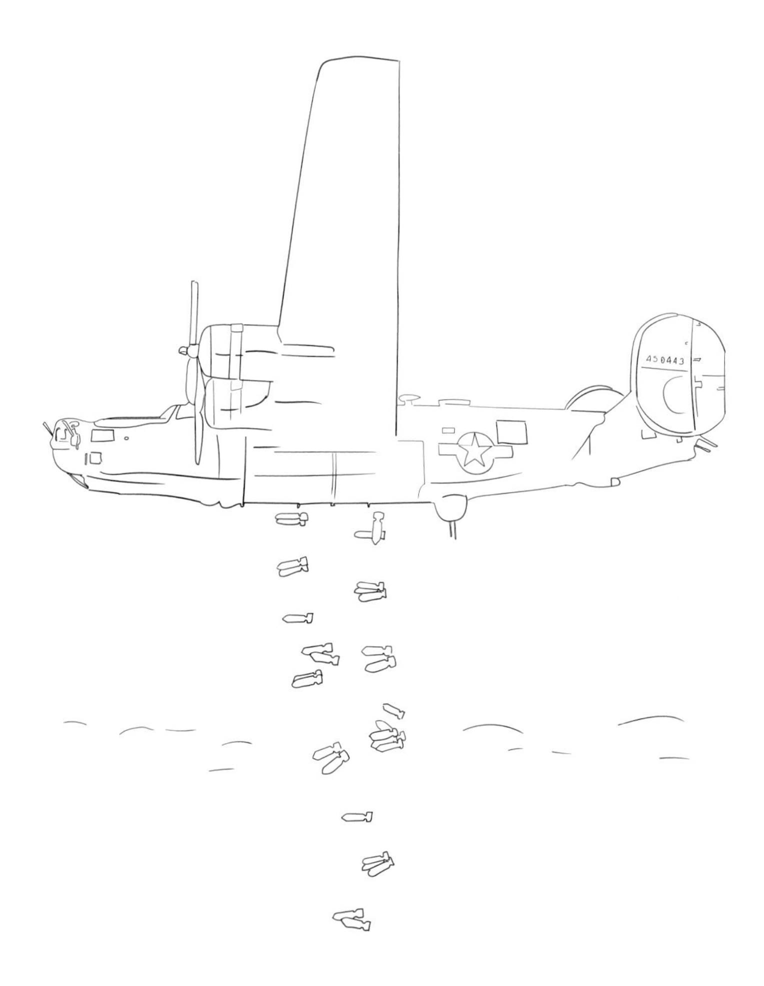

I am writing this at 14:56 on 8th May. Seventy-five years ago, in exactly four minutes time to be precise, Prime Minister Winston Churchill made an announcement on the radio that, following Germany's surrender the day before, the war in Europe had come to an end. One can only imagine the unbridled joy that this brought to the people of our country. In fact, I don't need to imagine, my mother and father fought in the war, and they told me. They fought for what they believed was a just cause and risked their lives. At least my Dad did, stationed as he was in the North Africa with the RAF, where I am led to believe, from his late-night reminiscences, that he almost single-handedly gave Rommel a bloody nose. I got the impression my Mum had much more fun as a WREN up in Scotland, where, from the little I could glean from her, she seemed to mainly enjoy going to parties with lots of GIs. If they were alive, I am sure they would be celebrating today, and with good cause. Fascism was an evil that had to be defeated, and they played their small parts. I salute them, and salute the war veterans who survived and who should have been at the Cenotaph today to remember their fallen colleagues.

But history of wars is written by the winners, and the history of the second war has been writ large in legend and in Hollywood. What is missing is the part played by the West in the terribleness of the war and its aftermath. What is missing is our part in that evil, and perhaps VE Day is as appropriate a day as any to shine a light on this. Victory over Nazism came with its very own Holocaust, one of Western making, and was perpetrated by people guilty of some of the worst crimes in humanity.

Much is made of the body count in the Coronavirus War. As of today, it is estimated at two hundred and seventy-six thousand worldwide. Which is tragic - of course it is. But some estimates of the death toll due to Allied bombing in Dresden just before the VE day, incredibly, put the numbers of dead at very similar levels. One small city, over just a few days. A city that had no political, military or industrial significance. Its population of six hundred thousand people had been swelled by a further half a million fleeing the Red Army advance. Most had gathered in the centre of town, which was where British bombers were specifically ordered that they should drop their bombs. Many congregated in the big parks in the city, and these were machine gunned by American fighter planes the following day, who allegedly flew at heights of no more than twenty metres to make sure they shot as many fish in the barrel as possible. There is a vast discrepancy in the estimate of deaths - or murders - at Dresden. It is hard to find anything in the BBC archives that puts it at over twenty-five thousand. But again, history is written by the victors. If you read the testimony of survivors and witnesses - like Kurt Vonnegut, who went on to write Slaughterhouse Five - it is hard to imagine three quarters of the population actually survived - let alone ninety-eight per cent as the BBC would have it. The firestorm generated was so hot, apparently, that groups of people sheltering in cellars literally melted into a single block of lard. And that's not an image I imagine many of us want to celebrate today.

And at the end of the war things got worse. Under the Yalta agreement Russia received vast stretches of German and Polish territory in the East and, in recompense, Poland absorbed large tracts of the former Reich in the West, including much of Prussia, Pomerania and Silesia. What such decisions gave rise to was chillingly revealed by Winston Churchill. When a Polish official expressed doubt that such a massive uprooting of people could be carried out, the British prime minister is reported to have said, 'Don't mind the five or more million Germans. Stalin will see to them. You will not have trouble with them: they will cease to exist.'

It was, in fact, sixteen million Germans who were driven from their homes in the largest ethnic cleansing in history. To add to the famine this displacement caused, the Allies imposed laws which inflicted forced and premeditated starvation that is estimated to have killed over six million of them. One and a half million Germans were transported to Russia to be executed or worked to death - with British soldiers helping put them on the death trains. The Allies presided over the most extensive and systematised rape of a female population in history. American occupation troops were issued with fifty million condoms a month. Fifty million! If they were all used that would mean every German woman between the age of sixteen and sixty was raped almost every week by the Yanks alone, let alone the French and the Russians.

Anyone who has doubts that this was a systematic murder and violation of the defeated German people should read a book called *German is our Problem* by Henry Morgenthau Junior. Morgenthau, Roosevelt's Secretary of the Treasury, called for the complete destruction of Germany after the victory had been won. In addition to the dismantling or destruction of German industry and the permanent closure of mines, the Morgenthau Plan called for a reduction of the Reich's land area by one half. As many calculated, and as Roosevelt, and other proponents of the plan well knew, this act guaranteed that roughly two-thirds of the German population would soon die of starvation. With the remnant of the population reduced to subsistence farming, and with the shrunken nation totally at the mercy of hostile European neighbours, it was estimated that within two generations Germany would cease to exist. On September 15th, 1944, US President Franklin D. Roosevelt made the demand for extermination official when he endorsed the so-called Morgenthau Plan. 'We have got to be tough with Germany and I mean the German people, not just the Nazis.' Roosevelt is reported to have assured Henry Morgenthau. 'You either have to castrate the German people or you have got to treat them in such a manner so they can't go on reproducing.'

And on the shop-floor, this sentiment was very much endorsed. 'The German is a beast.' asserted General Dwight D. Eisenhower, Supreme Allied Commander in Europe. Not only would he give the Morgenthau Plan his whole-hearted support, he would personally do his utmost to kill as many Germans - soldiers and civilians - as he possibly could.

From the firebombing of Hamburg in 1943 to the firebombing of Dresden in 1945, the goal of the British RAF and the US Eighth Air Force was not only to gain military advantage, but to kill every man, woman and child in every German city and town. Likewise, from their first footfall into Germany, the goal of the Red Army in the East and the American army in the West, was to rape, and often murder, every woman they caught, to kill or enslave all the men they captured, and to destroy or steal virtually everything German they could find.

I try to teach my three boys that, win or lose, it is important to do both with equal grace. Sadly, there was very little grace in our victory in WWII to point at to support this lesson on VE Day. Apart from my Dad, of course, and the millions like him who died and risked their lives, only for our leaders to besmirch their bravery with the atrocities carried out in their name.

9TH MAY - EXIT STRATEGY

Boris smoothed down his hair. He hadn't quite got over the Thatcher influence, and had even found himself thinking about ironing his truss earlier in the day. The others filed in to the Cabinet Room and looked at him expectantly. 'So, 'ow are yous feelin' lad?' enquired Thérèse Coffey from beneath her fringe. Seven weeks of self-isolating had brought back her old Merseyside accent, as well as making her look remarkably like a labradoodle. 'Any news on when de footie is gonna start again?'

As normal, Boris completely ignored her. He was not too sure why he appointed her in the first place, but he had needed another bloody woman for the equality numbers, and no one else in their right mind had wanted to be Minister for Pensions. Baroness Evans sat next to Boris and took hold of his hand. 'I do hope you're feeling better Prime Minister.' she said earnestly.

'Who are you?' queried Boris, a bit concerned that one of the secretaries had gate-crashed the meeting.

'Natalie, Prime Minister. Natalie Evans.' she replied, slightly taken aback.

'Bloody loved you in Eastenders, Nat. But what are you doing at Cabinet? Did I put you in charge of culture?'

'I'm Leader of the House of Lords, Prime Minster,' glowered Baroness Evans, not a little put out at this stage, 'and Lord Privy Seal.'

'Gosh, you have done well since you gave that Ricky the heave-ho. Loved the show, but you can't sit there I'm afraid, old girl. That seat's taken.'

Just then Priti Patel stormed through the door, her Permanent Secretary following behind her, small droplets of blood dripping from a fairly recently inflicted wound. Baroness Evans had barely had time to start rising from her chain before Priti had wrapped her arm around her neck and sent her hurling to the floor. Priti motioned to her Permanent Secretary to upright the chair. 'Good morning, Prime Minister.' she said sweetly, though her pretty smile was betrayed by the icy burning of her cold, cold eyes. 'About time you stopped lounging around in bed, leaving all the work to the rest of us.'

Boris chortled, though not convincingly. There was something of the Norman Tebbit in this woman that frightened him. 'You do make me laugh Priti.' he said, trying not to sound too much like he was clenching his enormous buttocks as much as he actually was. He looked around the table to find someone who made him feel less nervous, and managed to catch the eye of Liz Truss. 'God, she looks hot.' thought Boris. Even though she had behaved disgracefully bringing Margaret back to life in an attempt to topple him, he couldn't bear a grudge for too long. Not when she looked this smoking. 'Hi there Elizabeth, and how are you today? Any idea when Rishi is going to get here?'

'He shouldn't be too long Prime Minister, I think he's just finishing his online schooling, and his teacher said he could leave before prep. Let's hope he's here soon. I'm so looking forward to hearing about your exit strategy Prime Minister. Everyone is.' she fluttered.

'Exit strategy?' asked Boris.

'Yes, Prime minister. The whole country is waiting to find out.'

'Well I can't do it straight away, can I?' said Boris. 'To be honest, I thought I would give it a while. It wouldn't look good if I did it straight away, not after everything that's happened.'

'Very wise, Prime Minister.' said Hancock earnestly. 'We need to protect our NHS. How long were you thinking?'

'A couple of years maybe.' mused Boris.

There was stunned silence around the Cabinet Office. 'A couple of years?' spluttered Alok Sharma. 'But what about business?'

‘Don’t you worry about that, Alok,’ winked Boris. ‘there will plenty of business going on. If you get my meaning.’

‘But how? If it’s like this for the next two years, the country will go to pot.’ remonstrated Raab, a worrying image floating across his mind of it being his turn at the daily briefing the day this was announced.

‘Well I think that’s a bit of overkill. Two years is a long time. Besides, there will be lots of parties to sneak off to. I’m not talking about being grounded the whole time.’

‘Parties? If there’s going to be parties, what’s your position on social distancing then Prime Minister?’ asked Robert Jenrick, pompously, keen to finally say something at Cabinet, even though nobody actually knew who he was.

‘Well you know me Rick.’ chuckled Boris, at least getting a bit of the name right, ‘I can play it as cool as the next man. If one needs to keep some distance to get the old interest going, I’m that man’.

‘But Boris, people are going to go mad. They will be tearing up the streets.’ protested Priti Patel - though secretly she was rather looking forward to ordering the police out in riot gear. And maybe disguising herself as Old Bill and getting stuck in herself.

‘And what about the schools?’ enquired Gavin Williamson. ‘We have to think about education above all.’

‘Don’t you worry about schooling Gavin old buddy. It’s all sorted, The name’s down with the old alma mater already.’ breezed Johnson cheerily.

'Boris, honestly, think about this. What's the reaction of the public going to be? This could cost us the next election.' pleaded Raab.

'Well I don't see why Dominic. It's not the nineteenth century you know. People will accept all kinds of things these days. Harry married a black woman, for heaven's sake, and people were fine with that. No - bad example. But you know what I mean. Look, I know everyone likes Carrie, but let me tell you, she's a complete cow. Wouldn't even have a three-upsie with Margaret when she was around. I mean, I ask you? Who would say 'no' to that? No, a couple of years will be fine. Provided I drag it out, it will be yesterday's news before we know what.' opined the Prime Minister confidently.

'So, just so we are absolutely clear, Prime Minister,' said Priti with some awe in her voice, 'we're not talking about the exit strategy for dealing with the lockdown, but about how you dump the woman who gave birth to your son a few days ago in the most politically expedient way.' Even by Priti's very high standards this seemed borderline cruel.

'Yes, of course. I thought that's why we were all meeting today. It is a bloody Saturday after all.'

A hint of desperation was detectable in Matt Hancock's voice. 'OK, you do what you want with your bird, but what do we do about the lockdown?'

'Oh. fuck that for a game of soldiers.' chuckled Boris. 'I've had the bloody disease, so I'm OK. Everyone else can go back to work on Monday. Now chaps,' he said, looking at his watch. 'I really should be down at Chequers playing wankers with Wigbert and Figgy, so I'm off.'

12TH MAY - THE THREE RS

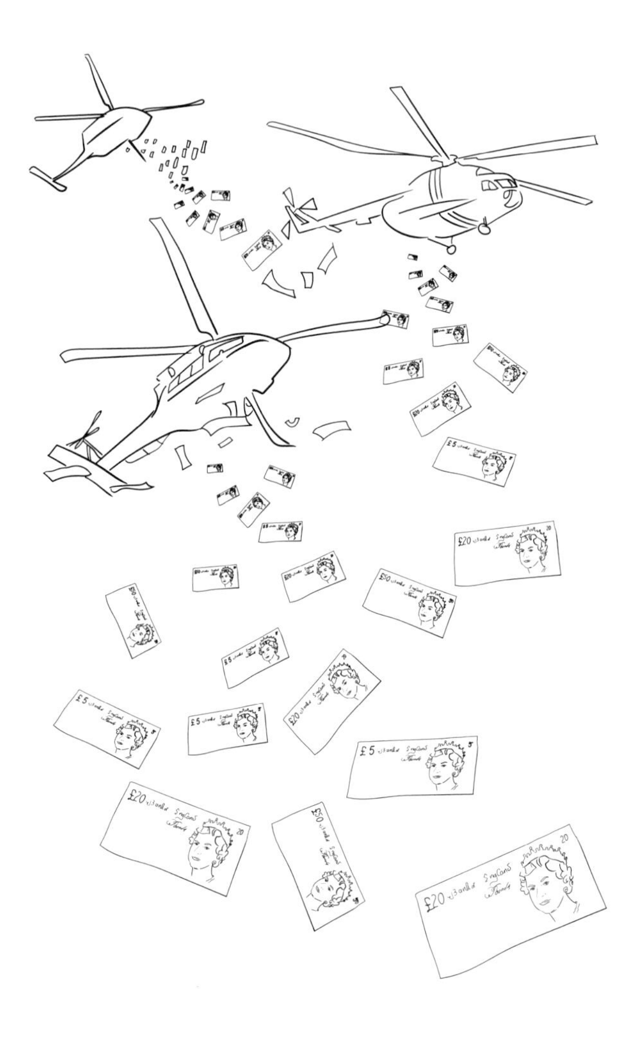

With schools being closed, there is rightly much concern for the impact on education. I have children, so this is a worry, but, in truth, I am less anxious about them not getting their quota of the three educational Rs than I am about three completely different Rs.

There is much talk of how we 'restart' the economy. Of the world sinking into depression, and of catastrophic job losses. The UK is said to be looking at a thirty-five per cent fall in GDP this quarter - this is - for once, quite literally - an unprecedented drop.

Helicopter Money is not a new idea, it was first mooted by Margaret Thatcher's favourite monetarist, Milton Friedman, in 1969. The idea is for a country's central bank to print money and drop it out of helicopters for people to pick up and spend, generating demand, and in turn growth. In reality, of course, they wouldn't actually drop it out of helicopters - though as I live two miles from the RAF Benson, which is home to two Puma squadrons, I think this would be a jolly good idea personally. Though I guess that, in these days of social distancing, encouraging us all outside to tear each other's hair out over stray £20 notes, maybe doesn't seem such a great idea. But more judiciously applied - distributing money to everyone through their bank accounts, for instance, would certainly be possible.

The normal objection to Helicopter Money is that a country doing it will suffer worsening exchange rates with other currencies, as these adjust to the artificial money supply, and this in turn leads to the rise in price of imported goods, and ultimately to spiralling inflation. But the whole world is now in the same position, and if - for once - the world united and acted as one, we could perhaps solve our problem overnight. If every country in the world agreed that every other country print a proportion of its GDP (say twenty-five per cent) in extra cash, but only on the basis that this was distributed in a prescribed manner - say forty per cent as an equal payment to every citizens directly, forty per cent to support businesses most affected by the pandemic, and twenty per cent to environmentally positive infrastructure projects to combat global warming - then we could kill lots of birds with one stone. And have no net effect on any one country's finances in relation to any other.

The left would hate it of course. I can already hear the horror in Corbynista voices that equal amounts of money are being given to everyone, rather than just to their vote base. They would, as normal, be completely missing the point. The purpose of this is not to right perceived inequity, but to get the economy going. Lots of businesses target wealthier people, who I imagine would be as happy as poorer people to pop out and spend their free dividend. It would almost certainly guarantee that the Tories won the next election, since nothing wins a vote more than a freebie. Which would be good obviously - not necessarily so we have more of Boris - it would just be great watch to see Keir Starmer actually explode with pomposity and indignation on primetime TV.

It won't happen of course. The UN can't agree on even simple things. Oddly, the Ruskies might be keener than one would normally expect, as all their oil money is evaporating. But now China has got the virus under control, with very little impact on its economy, the very last thing it would want to do is help the Yanks sort out their issues. And as those clever Chinese control and influence large parts of the world now, it wouldn't just be them on the side-lines, but all their cohorts and dependants too.

R IS FOR REPRODUCTION

Poor old Boris has been pelted with derision since his talk on Sunday. He has been accused of being imprecise, of blustering and of not knowing what he is doing. I have some sympathy with him - it's a tricky thing he's trying to deal with. And for a chap who studied classics, all this reliance on science must be jolly tedious. Part of it is presentational of course, although I thought his speech was actually pretty good, if I'm honest, and I don't really agree that there were that many mixed messages. Why people should berate him for telling people to go back to work if they can't work at home, but to try not to use public transport if they have other means of getting to work, is quite beyond me. It seems eminently sensible, but I detect that the health and safety police are starting to tie up their hobnailed boots - and in their eyes nothing can possibly be allowed to happen if there is an iota of associated risk. Maybe, when the helicopters have finished dropping their cash, we could have them crash land on Health & Safety HQ? There would be a rather delicious irony in that I feel.

Anyhow, back to Boris' speech. If he had said as his parting comment, 'And now we are publishing the detail behind what I have just said so everyone has absolute clarity on the rules.' that would have gone a long way to defuse the criticism. Even better, if he had explained the rationale better behind the rules, he would have got more buy-in. For instance, 'The reason you should only meet with one person in a public space is that the more people who are in a group, the harder it is to keep two metres apart.' And perhaps added, 'I understand that many of you might be able to keep social distancing with a group of three, but not everyone will, so as we are really trying our best to put in place rules that give us the best chances of getting out of this with the least damage. And our best chance is be to have a one rule for all approach. So please, please abide by it.' People buy into things when they better understand the reasons - they don't like being just told that, 'The science is telling us to do this.' Nobody trusts the bloody science, Boris - it was those scientist jonnies in the lab in Wuhan that got us into this in the first place.

The scientists' touchstone would appear to me to be the 'R' number. I suspect they think calling it 'R' rather than 'Effective Reproduction' number makes it sound a bit more James Bond. That, and I don't suppose they could call it the 'E' number, or we would definitely have some mixed messages going on. But am I the only one who can't square the quest for a low R number with the call for more testing? Let me explain my logic, and tell me if I am talking nonsense.

1. At the moment we only know whether someone has the virus if they get a test.

2. Other than NHS workers, people typically only get a test if they have the symptoms of the disease.

3. The more people we test the more people we will know are infected.

4. A great many people don't exhibit the symptoms of the disease, or do so in a very mild way. I have seen estimates by 'scientists' that between two and twenty million people have been infected - which isn't exactly a normal scientific margin for error.

5. Therefore, the more tests we do the more positive cases we will have.

6. Since we will then have more certified cases today than we did yesterday, the R number will go up!

7. So, to get the R number down, the best thing to do is stop testing.

Bingo! Problem solved. I am genuinely confused by this. If the only way of establishing the R number is by knowing definitively how many people are getting this afresh - and it would seem that we can't do this without testing everybody regularly - then the R number has little meaning. Confused? Maybe it's just me.

R IS FOR THE RIGHTEOUS BRIGADE

These are the people who form, and justify, their attitudes and opinions entirely based on their own prejudices and self-interest. They are the searchers for the moral high ground: the smug and the ignorant. Where to start? I mentioned the Health & Safety mob earlier. If I hear one more person trumpet out the old, 'we have to put people's health and safety in front of everything else chant.' I think I will explode. In normal life, we try to strike a balance between risk and reward. It's why we stopped people walking in front of cars with flags to warn pedestrians about the car, and why we allow people to smoke, even though smoking will kill two or three times as many people in the UK this year as Covid-19. But Health & Safety is insidious in modern life, and I have a feeling that, in Covid-19, it has found a fertile ground to sow its seed. This constant Health & Safety mantra is a virus all of its own, infecting us and destroying reason and logic. I am heartily sick of listening to the endless self-serving debates about the advisability of restarting the Premier League, for instance, and of footballers being concerned about their welfare. 'The majority of players are scared because they have children and families.' whimpered Sergio Aquero. Covid-19 is essentially an old person's disease, Sergio. Out of ten million under-fives in Britain, just two have died. For under-twenty-fives, the risk is one or two per million - less than a bunch of diseases people have never heard of. Go and bloody have a game of football mate, and cheer us all up. Preferably by missing a penalty against Liverpool.

Next up we have the haters of middle-class white men. Who are often, it would seem, middle-class white men. A huge amount has been made about people of black and middle-eastern origin having higher death rates than white people, and this is now going to be subject to an 'Inquiry'. The Office for National Statistics has concluded that Black people are 1.9 times more likely to die than white people, Bangladeshis and Pakistanis are 1.8 times more likely, and Indians are around 1.5 times more likely. The Left, it would appear, would have us believe that this is some form of conspiracy and represents how badly these 'communities' are treated in our racist country. Let me save the money of the Inquiry - we can pop it into the helicopter fund. Here are three pretty good contributing reasons the disparity on numbers of deaths which might sit behind the headlines:

1. Black people are more likely to be overweight than white people. This is a statistical fact, not a racist observation, and is confirmed in the government's own report on 'Overweight Adults'. This therefore puts a greater number of black people in a high-risk group.

2. Both Asian and black populations have been found to have a significantly higher risk of diabetes and heart disease, according to the IFS, putting a far greater number in the high-risk category. At-risk underlying health conditions are especially prevalent among older Bangladeshis, Pakistanis and black Caribbeans. Compared with white British individuals over sixty years of age, Bangladeshis are more than sixty per cent more likely to have a long-term health condition that makes them particularly vulnerable to infection.

3. BAME families tend to be bigger, and live in densely populated areas, so people are more exposed to other people generally. The average Muslim family, I am led to believe, has twice as many children as the average UK family. They also have a (rather enviable) culture where multiple generations of a family will live in the same house - in all likelihood exposing their older people more to the risk of infection.

The Institute of Fiscal Studies actually concluded that, if we look at both geography and age combined, the death rate for BAME might actually be lower for most ethnicities than for white people based on age demographics, Still, if all you ever see and hear are things that confirm your prejudices, you are almost certainly prejudiced, and you will give about as much credence to these facts as you would to Meghan Markle saying how much she misses England. What I find especially intriguing in all this is that there would appear to be a fifty per cent greater chance of dying if you're bloke and not a woman, but I haven't heard a single voice clamouring for an Inquiry over this blatantly sexist targeting of men by the virus!

15TH MAY - THE MERCHANT OF LITTLE VENICE

Borisanio stared out at the Regent's Canal. 'How much wage doth we hath left, mine own cousin?' he asked glumly.

'Wherefore mast'r, we art doen to our last ducat.' replied young Rishi, his manservant. 'We hath spent ev'ry last penny paying f'r furloughing. Thine well is dry.'

Borisanio stood up. His chin jutted out. Or at least the top one jutted out over the other three. 'Then we has't nay alternative. If 't be true I am to winneth the affections of lovely China, I wouldst hide mine own pride and borrow wage from whosever shall lendeth to me.' And, with this, he turned and walked purposefully towards St. John's Wood.

Whilst Borasanio was contemplating his pecunious state, Shycock was holding court at Richmond House. 'Gentleman, we has't achieved a most wondrous thing. For many years our most wondrous NHS hast been starved of funds. Anon we all liveth in fear, and everyone loves every last nurse and every last doctor who keepeth folk alive. We hath persuaded the child Rishi to giveth us every penny of taxpayers wage to combat this plague, and anon the state shall never again deny us.' With this he turned to the massive gilt framed picture of Nye Bevan, and raised his glass his to his followers. 'Drinketh and beest merry mine own cousins. The present day we hath wonneth the war'.

Borisanio finally arrived at the bike station. Somewhat out of breath after his walk and recent confinement in hospital, he searched his pockets for the last of his coppers, pushed it into the slot, and cycled towards Richmond House. The wind blew his blonde locks behind him as a mist rose from the Thames to engulf Olde London Town, so that his bulky shadow no longer stretched out onto the cobbled street, but was lost, like his soul, in the night air.

By the time he had arrived at Whitehall, Borisanio had made up his mind. Whatever Shycock asked of him he would give. He must have three thousand dukats to fund his flagship road to the North, and now that buffoon Sunak had given everything to the NHS, Shycock was the man with the money. This was his one chance to save his premiership, and not be forever written off as history's clown. He summoned up all his courage, and grasped the knocker.

The loud banging disturbed the revelry in Richmond House. Christopher Whitty came up for air from the ample bosom of a nurse from St Thomas. 'Who doth thee bethink yond might beest Matthew.' he spluttered.

'I hast nay idea, but unless he hath a key workers pass there is nay entry to this party.' said Shycock haughtily. 'Girls, putteth on thy clothing and seeth who is't at the door.' he demanded.

Liz and Priti did as bid, and wrapped the minimum of clothing around their supple bodies. When the door swung open, Borisanio was confronted with the sight of his two minsters learning drunkenly against the arch. 'What endues thee here bacon-fed knave?' asked Priti, her eyes empty as an Everton trophy cabinet.

Borisanio looked at her with distain. 'Thee didst betray me Priti, and thee Elizabeth.' he declared, pushing past them into the thick of the party. Two Siamese twins were taking it in turn to pleasure Dominic Rabb. 'Fair enough.' thought Borisanio, who could see this was a temptation no reasonable man could resist. 'Shycock', he demanded. 'Alloweth us talketh. In private, prithee.'

Borisanio and Shycock retired to an antechamber. 'I needeth three thousand dukets, Matthew.' demanded the Prime Minister. 'Nameth thy terms'.

Shycock laughed disdainfully. 'And wherefore wouldst I lendeth wage to thee Borisanio. Thee hast nothing left. I hast everything anon.'

'Thou art wrong sir. I hast one last thing. I hast two ships, sailing from Scotland replete with north sea oil. I shall payeth thee back in short order.'

'Tis fine then Borisanio. Thee has't three months to repay me. But if 't be true thee faileth to beest here on this day in three months to repay me, I shall insist yond I taketh a pound of thy flesh from closest to thine heart by way of penalty. Doth thee concur?'

'Aye, I concur sir.' Borisanio agreed, and turned and stalked out of the building, stopping only to grope a particularly perky pair of boobs that a dark lady was wobbling in the general direction of the lute player in the string quartet.

Three months passed by, and Borisanio was becoming increasingly concerned as no sighting of his ships had been made. He woke to a drizzly dawn on the final day for repayment of his loan, and looked across at Carrie. 'This might beest mine own last day on this earth, mine own love.' he said plaintively. Just then there was a loud hammering on the door of Number 10. 'I seeth them my lord, I seeth them.' he heard Rishi shouting excitedly. Borisanio jumped out of bed and pulled on his beeches. 'Alloweth us wend meeteth them mine own cousin.' he said, pushing Rishi into his carriage. 'To the docks driver.' he instructed.

Ten minutes later the pair were at the banks of the Thames. Two particularly large and unattractive ships, *The Dirty Nicola* and *The Slutty Sturgeon*, were indeed heading down the Thames. Borisanio was almost bursting with relief, when he heard a familiar voice behind him. 'So Borisanio, thee shall repay me this present day?'

'Shycock, thee can seeth I hast two ships replete with oil. I can payeth thee with interest.' retorted Borisanio.

Shycock turned to the man next to him. 'Merchant, bid me, what be the price of oil on the market this present day?'

'Sir, the price of oil hast collapsed with this plague, thee wouldst giveth me dukets to taketh it off thy hands.'

Shycock smirked, as Borisanio turned as pale as an albino on a ventilator. 'A pound of flesh sir, from closest to thine heart.' he demanded with a sneer.

Just then the Lord Chief Justice for England and Wales, John Thomas, arrived. 'Shycock, I understand thee requireth Borisanio to giveth thee a pound of flesh from the part of his corse closest to his heart? I will concur this be fair request, as Birisanio hast signed a contract, but thee must ensureth he doest not loseth a single drop of blood. So this operation must taketh lodging in a hospital of the state, and the law requires this befall within one year of this day.'

Shycock's smirk disappeared from his face. 'One fine day sir, I shalt hath revenge.' he glowered at Borisanio. With the waiting list for elective surgery now at over seven million, he knew well this operation could never be scheduled in so short a time.

19TH MAY - AMERICAN LIE

A long long time ago
I can still remember how
His speeches used to make me smile
But I knew if I had my chance
I would make that bastard dance
And maybe I'd be happy for a while
Then February made me shiver
With every press briefing he'd deliver
Bad news on the doorstep
People who couldn't take one more step
I'm pretty sure he never cried

When he read about those widowed brides
Nothing touched him deep inside
The day the virus arrived

So
Bye, bye Miss American Pie
Drove my Chevy to the levee but the levee was dry
And them good ole boys were drinking whiskey and rye
Singin' this'll be the day that I die
This'll be the day that I die

And did you write the book of lies
And should we never show surprise
If Fox News tells us so
Should we believe you, Donald Trump
That bleach will save our mortal rump?
And can you teach us how to die real slow?
Well, you know we were betrayed by you
'Cause you left us dyin' in the ICU
You just kicked off your shoes
And lit the pandemic fuse
You're a fat orange lying fuck
With a pink carnation and a funeral truck
And I knew we were out of luck
The day the virus arrived

I started singin'
Bye, bye Miss American Pie
Drove my Chevy to the levee but the levee was dry
And them good ole boys were drinking whiskey and rye
Singin' this'll be the day that I die
This'll be the day that I die

Now, for four years you've been out on your own
The poor growing poorer as the rich have grown
And that's not how it used to be
When the jester sang for the queen and king
In a coat he borrowed from James Dean
In a voice that represented all of us
Oh but while the king was looking down
You stole his thorny crown
The courtroom was adjourned
No verdict was returned
And while this nation lost its spark
We protested in the park
And you sang dirges of the dark
the day the virus arrived

We were singin'
Bye, bye Miss American Pie
Drove my Chevy to the levee but the levee was dry
Them good ole boys were drinking whiskey and rye
And singin' this'll be the day that I die
This'll be the day that I die

Helter skelter in a summer swelter
We're all looking for a fallout shelter
Eighty thousand and growing fast
The bodies piled out on the grass
You try again for a forward pass
With the jester on the sidelines in a cast.
Now the half-time air was death perfume
While lackys played your marching tune
We all got up to dance
Oh, but we never got the chance

'Cause time and again you refused to yield
And our fate was well and truly sealed
Do you recall what was revealed
The day the virus arrived?

We started singin'
Bye, bye Miss American Pie
Drove my Chevy to the levee but the levee was dry
Them good ole boys were drinking whiskey and rye
And singin' this'll be the day that I die
This'll be the day that I die

Oh, and there we were all in one place
A generation lost in space
With no time left to start again
So Don be nimble, Don be quick
Donald Trump the people's pick
But lies are the devil's only friend
Oh and as I watched you on the stage
My hands were clenched in fists of rage
No angel born in Hell
Could break that Satan's spell
And as the flames climbed high into the night
To light the sacrificial rite
I saw Satan laughing with delight
The day the virus arrived

He was singin'
Bye, bye Miss American Pie
Drove my Chevy to the levee but the levee was dry
Them good ole boys were drinking whiskey and rye

Singin' this'll be the day that I die
This'll be the day that I die

I met a girl who sang the blues
And I asked her for some happy news
But she just smiled and turned away
I went down to the sacred store
Where I'd heard the music years before
But the man there said the music wouldn't play
And in the streets the children screamed
The lovers cried, and the poets dreamed
But not a word was spoken
The church bells all were broken
And the three men I admire most
The Father, Son, and the Holy Ghost
They caught the last train for the coast
The day the virus arrived

And they were singing
Bye, bye Miss American Pie
Drove my Chevy to the levee but the levee was dry
And them good ole boys were drinking whiskey and rye
Singin' this'll be the day that I die
This'll be the day that I die
They were singing
Bye, bye Miss American Pie
Drove my Chevy to the levee but the levee was dry
Them good ole boys were drinking whiskey and rye
Singin' this'll be the day that I die

20TH MAY - I SCREAM, YOU SCREAM, WE ALL SCREAM FOR VACCINE

On 15th April 1989 one of the worst football disasters in sporting history occurred at the FA Cup semi-final between Liverpool and Nottingham Forest, when ninety-six Liverpool Fans were crushed to death at Hillsborough. It was an event that burned itself on the city of Liverpool. There was almost nobody bought up there who didn't know a family who was affected, and the *Families of the 96* have been fighting for justice ever since. In November this year, thirty years on, justice was finally denied when, in a re-trial, South Yorkshire Police match commander, David Duckenfield, was found not guilty of gross negligence manslaughter. But the repercussions of the disaster were further-reaching than our inability to call senior people to account for their actions that day. In the aftermath of disaster, the government commissioned a report by Lord Justice Taylor. The Taylor Report, as it is known, found that the main reason for the disaster was the failure of police control. The report stated that, 'Whilst standing accommodation is not intrinsically unsafe, all-seater stadia bring benefits to spectator comfort, safety and crowd control.' Indeed none of the reports into crowd safety in the twentieth century had ever found any inherent danger in standing on the terraces, and standing areas are still permitted today in the lower leagues provided they meet regulatory standards. The government, however, in the way that governments will, decided that no standing accommodation was to be allowed at all. They saw this as being a handy way of addressing the hooligan problems that had beset football, and of making crowds easier to monitor and control.

Since then many senior figures in the game, such as Jose Mourinho and Arsene Wenger, have come out as massively in favour of safe-standing areas. Indeed, a recent survey showed that nineteen of the twenty current Premier League clubs say they would actively support safe standing if legislation allowed it. I watched the Liverpool Champions League tie against Atletico Madrid in March standing on the Anfield Kop with my son, Anthony. Standing? Yes, standing. Not a single person on the Kop sat down for the vast majority of the game. Anthony had to stand on his seat to watch, and without question the whole environment was far less safe than had we been in a designated standing area regulated with some safety in mind. Why have I suddenly gone off-piste and started rambling on about football safety? Well I think there are a couple of lessons we as a society might very well take from this, as we contemplate out reaction to this pandemic and how it will change the world going forward.

The first is that, once given away, freedoms are very hard to win back. We don't need to look at football to see this, the history of the twentieth century is of countries and people oppressed under fascism and communism. The misery caused by both dogmas has been incalculable, but whilst they are often portrayed as being at opposite ends of the ideological spectrum, both were founded on suppression of individual freedom.

The second is that there is nothing quite like a disaster to create a climate where people are prepared to sacrifice those freedoms. Whether out of fear or outrage, people will accept new norms and new rules more willingly and more compliantly when crisis rears its head. The disaster of the burning of the Reichstag in 1933 was the single event above all others that brought Hitler to ultimate power, for instance. Carried along on a wave of outrage he expelled the communists from the Parliament and imprisoned their leaders. A state of emergency was declared which resulted in newspapers being censored and personal letters and phone calls being checked. This was the start of the end of democracy in Germany. The rest, as they say, is history.

So, where are the parallels today? Well let's start off with vaccination. Vaccination is the great white hope for our future, with several minsters being quoted as saying we can't hope to go back to full normality until we have a vaccine to inoculate everyone with. Now I'm not an anti-vaccinator per se, and I would dearly love there to be a silver bullet solution to all this madness, but I certainly had the wind taken out of my sails by an article I stumbled across from 2015 on the flu vaccine. The Royal College of General Practitioners had apparently warned that vaccination rates in October of that year were an 'alarming' six per cent lower, compared with the same time the previous year. The article went on to say that public confidence in the jab has been affected by the fact that the previous year's vaccine hadn't worked very well - scientists had identified the wrong strain of flu to target, apparently, and as a result the jab worked in a mere three per cent of cases. The figure was later revised up to thirty-four per cent, but I have to confess to being more than a little stunned at this. The NHS spends over a hundred million pounds a year on the national flu jab campaign, and even on the more optimistic assessment, two-thirds of this appeared to have been completely wasted. But thank heavens, along came the WHO to reassure me. In previous years, WHO experts confidently asserted, the jab's effectiveness rates had usually been around fifty per cent - meaning that close to half the people inoculated were protected against contracting flu that year. Well, that's a relief then! Here's me thinking it didn't work so well.

Let's roll this forward to how we are reacting to Covid-19 today. We have heard Trump tell us how we will have a vaccine by Xmas (just after the US election coincidentally), so we know that's a lie as we saw his lips moving, but let's assume he is right for once, and we have a vaccine. The logic of vaccination, as I understand it - as they seem not to work for quite a lot of people - is as much about driving 'herd immunity' as much as it is about individual protection. If a large enough section of the population can be vaccinated, the virus can't spread as easily, giving protection to those left unvaccinated. There is much talk of whether a Covid-19 vaccination will be made compulsory in order to drive herd immunity, and protect the many at the expense of the few vaccine-resisters. In other words, that we should take away an individual's choice of what medicines he puts into his body for the greater good. That is an ethical question in its own right, but if the vaccine we get is as effective as that for flu - if half the time it simply doesn't work - whether it's ethical or not is neither here nor there, it simply cannot meet its objective, given the virus' reproduction rate. At best it might temper the spread, but it seems unlikely that it will make it go away and allow us to return to normality. Answer me this, if you had been vaccinated today and knew it halved your chances of getting the disease, would you feel any safer? Would you think that was the moment to start embracing complete strangers in the street? I am guessing that. for many of us, the answer to this would be 'no!'

But the inadequacies of the flu jab are not the only issue. Around seven million Britons are currently taking statins - cholesterol-lowering drugs - and many of these are older people who are in high risk groups. Two major studies have warned that the statin pills seem to stop the flu jab working properly. When people on statins have the jab, they do not produce as many antibodies to the flu virus as normal. This means they may not be adequately protected against developing the illness. Dr Steven Black, a paediatric infectious diseases specialist at the Cincinnati Children's Hospital, found that among seven thousand over sixty-fives, statin users had a significantly reduced immune response to vaccines. This is supported by researchers at the Emory Vaccine Centre at Emory University in Atlanta, who found an increase in illness in vaccinated people who were taking statins. So, if this is mirrored in Covid-19, those people in the a group most likely to be badly affected by the virus are amongst the least likely to have success with the jab. And this says nothing about potential dangers of vaccination generally - particularly one rushed into the market after limited testing, as any Covid-19 vaccination will undoubtedly be. More than one hundred Britons are currently involved in a long-running legal battle for compensation for the narcolepsy (overpowering daytime sleepiness) that they blame on the Pandemrix vaccine - the jab rushed out to combat the swine flu epidemic in 2009. It has not been used since. In June, a twelve year-old British boy - whose narcolepsy has left him unable even to shower by himself - won a hundred and twenty thousand pounds in compensation after a three-year legal battle.

Dr Tom Jefferson is an honorary fellow of the Oxford University Centre for Evidence-Based Medicine. He's also a practicing GP and public health specialist whose expert field is respiratory infections. Dr. Jefferson is an author and editor of the world-renowned Cochrane Collaboration, an independent body that analyses research, and he has spent twenty years studying the research data on influenza vaccination. He believes passionately that the medical evidence does not justify flu jab campaigns. He asserts the vast majority of clinical studies have been badly run - they were too small, or too sloppy with their analysis, or too open to influence from pharmaceutical companies - and that the results from studies funded by pharmaceutical companies have only been released selectively to show positive results, and have been spun by drug company representatives to give the impression their vaccines are more effective than they actually are.

'There have been very few gold-standard studies, called randomised controlled trials (RCTs),' he says, 'the RCTs that have been performed don't change the picture very much. The flu inoculation is a poorly performing vaccine that is insufficiently studied...... The available studies showed that the people for whom the vaccines work best are healthy adults - who need them least.'

But, rest assured, the governments who belatedly rushed into closing the world down, rather than introducing timely common-sense measures to stop the coronavirus spreading like a bush fire, will be the first to embrace the silver bullet vaccine fix. They will pay over our money to the pharmaceutical companies, who stand to profit massively from sales of a vaccine, whether it works or not. And because the populace has been terrified into submission by this virus, it will accept this gladly - as well as all manner of other controls over it - in order to bring some respite to the fear that has infected the world with more widespread and lasting damage than the coronavirus itself.

Freedoms are normally eroded gradually. None of us, quite reasonably wants to give them up without a very good reason. Particularly to Governments and police forces, who don't have an exactly unblemished records of not abusing new powers. But there is nothing Jonny Control-Freak loves more than a crisis. It enables him to anoint himself emergency powers, which are very often hard to wrestle back. We need look no further than Viktor Orban in Hungary today to see how he has exploited this crisis to make himself all-powerful, and you would get long odds on him volunteering to give these powers up easily. I would like to think that, in the UK, we are not quite in this position but, by the same token, the idea of computerised tracking and tracing is decidedly unsettling. The police have for years wanted more powers and technology to control the populace. Often the reasons for wanting this are laudable - and justifiable for particular reasons, and when entrusted into the hands of decent people. But history tells us that there are lots of people who aren't decent, and when they gain possession of the laws and technology to control us, we move into a very dangerous world indeed. How far a step is it, for instance, from us agreeing to have the government track our phone, to being forced to wear tracking wristbands? Or to have chips inserted in us like pets? These are question that needs answers.

Am I against using technology to track the spread of the disease? Am I against vaccination? No, I don't think so. But I am very much against all of this being the thin end of the wedge. I am very much against the pandemic being exploited to further vested interests and agendas through fear. So, I will leave you with a parting thought. Why are perfectly healthy people being encouraged to wear masks the world over when there is little or no evidence that this makes a jot of difference? And to what degree do you think this creates a climate of other-worldliness, of a change in societal normality, that makes other changes easier for us to accept? Thirty years on, and we still don't have safe seating areas at football. Think on!

22ND MAY - NOMINATIONS

THE NOMINATIONS FOR BEST PANDEMIC MOVIES ARE:

Nomination: *Ricard Branson and Tim Martin*
Movie: *Dirty Rotten Scoundrels*

Nomination: *Vladimir Putin and Xi Jimping*
Movie: *The Usual Suspects*

Nomination: *The World Heath Organisation*
Movie: *Lost in Translation*

Nomination: *Looroll Hoarders*
Movie: *Dirty Harry*

Nomination: *Boris Johnson and Matt Hancock*
Movie: *No Country for Old Men*

Nomination: *Rishi Sunak*
Movie: *Goldfinger*

Nomination: *Donald Trump*
Movie: *American Psycho*

Nomination: *Corona Virus*
Movie: *Batman*

Nomination: *The staff of the NHS*
Movie: *Goodfellas*

Nomination: *The Pharmaceutical Industry*
Movie: *The Gold Rush*

AND THE NOMINATIONS FOR BEST PANDEMIC SOUNDTRACKS:

Nomination: *The Police*
Song: *Don't stand so close to me*

Nomination: *The Specials*
Song: *Ghost Town*

Nomination: *Berlin*
Song: *You take my breath away*

Nomination: *Tiffany*
Song: *I think we're alone now*

Nomination: *The Verve*
Song: *The drugs don't work*

Nomination: *Thin Lizzy*
Song: *There's a killer on the loose*

Nomination: *D Ream*
Song: *Things can only get better*

Nomination: *Johnny Kidd and the Pirates*
Song: *Shaking all over*

Nomination: *The Kinks*
Song: *You really got me*

Nomination: *The Beatles*
Song: *Help*

26TH MAY - BATTLES OF THE EGOS - CUMMINGS VS. MORGAN.

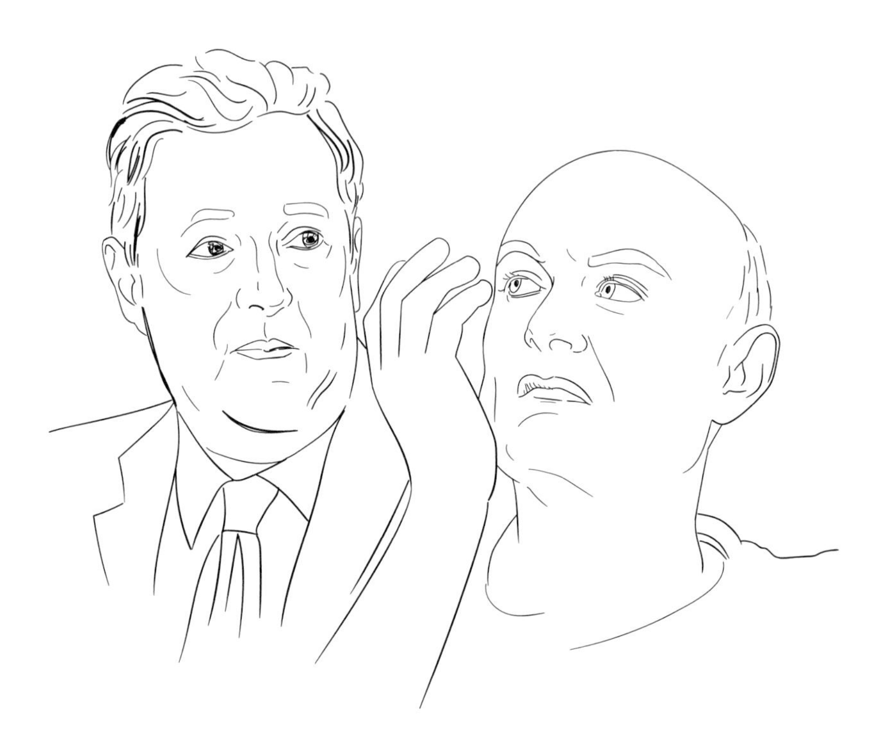

Now, don't get me wrong, I think Dominic Cummings is an odious little shit. Let's face it, he looks like a weaselly arrogant git, which doesn't help. And he has the personal charm of a Frenchman who has just run out of red wine, cheese and condoms. So, this has got to be a good moment, right? Seeing someone, who so clearly deserves it, having a dis-embowelling cutlass slowly working itself up his scrawny little butt must be a good thing? The comeuppance that he so clearly deserves. The various pillars of the establishment are lining up to cast their stones: the Church, the Police, the BBC, his own conservative MPs - the blighter is getting it from every angle. We were even treated to the quite astonishing sight of Alastair Campbell being interviewed on Channel 4 tonight, and heading off up to the moral high ground - rarified territory for him, of all people, to inhabit. The knives are out; by the time I have finished this post he may well have gone, encouraged to fall on his sword to protect the Prime Minister. Done the decent thing, as they say. Well, if that's the case, shame on all of us. He will be the victim not of his own behaviour, or of his inherent unpleasantness or lack of scruples, but of the sanctimony, self-righteousness and bear-baiting that has become the norm for how we conduct ourselves in this country. There is nothing about Dominic Cummings that doesn't make me want to bend him over and kick him very hard in his bony ass, but for all the things I dislike about him, that is not a just cause to invent a justification for so doing. There is a reason that a person's prior convictions aren't read out in court when they are up in front of the beak - it's so the jury isn't moved to convict someone based on past form, rather than on the evidence presented in the case. And the day that this changes will be a cold day in hell for justice in this country. But the same is certainly not true in the court of popular opinion. Cummings is being pilloried because he's a little shit - and because we desperately want to have a scapegoat for the perceived inadequacies of the government in recent months - not because the facts of the matter demand this. So, and it pains me to say this, give the bloke a bloody break!

What are the facts of the matter? Well, we're not sure, to be honest, as they seem under dispute. What seems clear, however, is that he drove up to Durham in order to park his little girl off somewhere she could be looked after properly. And while he was there, he popped out to have his eyes tested because these seemed to be playing up. Now, like it or not, Dominic Cummings plays a hugely important role in this government, and not even his worst enemies seem to deny that he's an extremely bright cookie. And with Boris off on his hols as a guest of the NHS, his role was, I am guessing, even more central at this critical time. So, my question is this. Would we rather have a key figure in our war against the pandemic fully focused on the job at hand - and ideally able to read the stuff put in front of him - or would we prefer his five-year old little girl was interrupting him every five minutes, and he couldn't make out from the report in front of him whether we were short of nurses or hearses? Yes, I get that we had set some rules, but the media behave, and much of the narrative unfolds, as though the rules are the end in themselves, rather than the means to the end. Let me ask you another question. If we hadn't been lucky enough to have had this pandemic at precisely the time the technology enabled video conferencing so easily, would we have been so insistent our leaders followed all the rules? Or might we have taken comfort in the idea that they were actually meeting up to work a way out of this mess, even though they were doing stuff we were being told not to? I certainly know what I would prefer.

Early on in this journal I posted a piece I called *The Blame Game*. Without sounding self-congratulatory, it was actually rather prescient. All we ever seem to hear, in the questioning of politicians and in the commentary on their actions, is an eternal quest for culpability. It is as though, if we can pin the blame on someone, we have solved the problem. We haven't. Indeed, we may well actually be compounding it, by distracting the very people we need to be focused, and having them spend their time justifying themselves to us. Of course, the government has made mistakes. Lots of them in my view. But much of the decisions have been judgement calls. We started off with herd immunity as the way forward, but that was clearly not going to be acceptable, so we changed tack, and lost time that may have moderated the effect of the virus had different decisions been made. But that's life. Who amongst us has never made a mistake? Put yourself in the place of the politicians being advised to do different things by different 'experts', and where whatever decision you make has massive negative repercussions? It's not a walk in the park - there was no playbook as a reference guide here. (Maybe there should have been one, but that's a different matter). What certainly doesn't help at all is having a self-congratulatory egotist, like Piers Morgan, building a reputation as the voice of the people on the back of being ridiculously aggressive and accusatory to the politicians he interviews. Let's not forget that is only six years since this man was sacked by the *Daily Mirror* for publishing fake pictures of British troops torturing Iraqis under the headline: 'Vile', amongst fears that this had endangered the lives of British troops in Basra. After a fortnight of recriminations, the Ministry of Defense declared that these pictures were fake and could not have been taken in Iraq. Colonel David Black, a former commanding officer of the accused regiment, said, 'It is time the ego of an editor is measured against the life of a soldier.' Let's not forget too that, until the writing on the wall became so big that even he couldn't ignore it, Piers boasted proudly of his friendship with Donald Trump. Piers Morgan: a man of judgement indeed. How easy it is to shout down and criticise that we haven't got enough PPE - at a time the whole world is short. How easy to criticise when you don't have peoples' lives, and the future of the country, in your hands.

I started off by saying that Dominic Cummings is an odious little shit, and I see no reason to retract that. I won't be asking him round to dinner any time soon, or offering to look after his little girl or hold his spectacles either. But if I had to choose which arse I would like to take a run up at and give a huge kick, I would definitely go for fleshy Morgan over bony Cummings any day of the week.

30TH MAY - A BRAVE NEW WORLD?

When we first went into lockdown many were saying that, when it was all over, the world would be a different place. It would come to its senses and recognise the folly of its ways. We would become nicer as people, more focused on the important things in life. And I can understand why people might think this. We stopped driving cars and flying planes, and the world suddenly seemed a cleaner place. We stopped trying to fit twenty-five hours into a twenty-four-hour day, and for the first time in many people's adult lives they had time to sit and reflect, rather than peddle ever faster on their hamster wheels. Maybe, many people thought, this mini apocalypse would come with a silver lining, which we could detach and use as our lead into a better world. Noble thoughts, of course they are, but I thought them naive then, and, ten weeks on, they look naiver still. The world we will go back to will, I fear, be scarier, more dangerous, less free and, frankly, a whole lot shitter than the one we left behind.

Early on in my journal (28th March), I did a piece on psychopaths and sociopaths, and the prevalence of such people in positions of power. I concluded by saying:

'So, where are we, what is the big picture? Well, it is this, A world that conducts itself based on an impossible growth strategy, run by people who, frankly, don't give a shit, and don't look at life like the rest of us. Against this backdrop, do you really see a changed world when we come out of this? I've told you my view. I hope the optimists amongst us are right, and I am wrong. I really do.'

I know you are just dying to go back and re-read the whole piece, but please, save that joy for later while I captivate you afresh. Having just promised captivation, probably the next word you expected to read was not 'economics' - but bear with me, it will get better I promise. Economics is typically looked at in two ways: macroeconomics, which looks at the systemic behaviour of the economy as whole, and microeconomics, which is broadly concerned with the effects and drivers of individual decisions. And that's all I'm going to say about economics, so it's already getting more fun. I just wanted to borrow from the economics dichotomy, and set the scene for looking at the world as we emerge from this pandemic from both a macro and micro perspective.

Let's start with the big picture - the macro-view of what is happening on our planet. Some four decades ago, Deng Xiao-ping took command of China, a country that had been nearly wrecked through Mao's radical Marxist experiments, such as the *Great Leap Forward* and the *Cultural Revolution*. Deng announced a new economic policy of *Socialism with Chinese characteristics*. Many in the West predicted that political liberalisation would soon follow the economic liberalisation initiated by Deng. Others were sceptical that the Communist Party would relinquish any meaningful degree of its political power, noting that Deng had stressed that, 'We shall adhere to Marxism and keep to the socialist road.' Now, a great thing about a totalitarian regime is that, provided it is not overthrown, it can play the long game. Our democracies are short affairs; governments are focused on the here and now - on making sure they stay popular enough to get elected next time around. It is really hard to have a long-term plan - and even harder to stick to it. The politics of compromise, of reacting to today's events in a populist way, is the politics of today, not of the long term. Another useful thing about a totalitarian regime is that it's a whole lot easier to suppress dissent. The demarcation lines which provide balance in a democratic society - rights, judiciary, electoral process - if they are drawn at all, are thinly drawn in a totalitarian state.

And China is a totalitarian regime that has played the long-game brilliantly. From the acquisition of Hong Kong, through buying up half of Africa, to building the world's second largest economy. And now their moment has come. Whilst the countries of the world have been looking inwards to fight a virus that originated in China, China has looked outwards. While our attention has been elsewhere, the democratic movement in Hong Kong is being crushed, Chinese troops are clashing with Indians on their disputed border, and there is a military buildup in the South China Sea. Most alarmingly the Chinese Belt and Road initiative is starting to find a foothold in Europe. *Belt and Road* is China's campaign for global dominance. President Xi Jinping announced his grand plan about five years ago to connect Asia, Africa and Europe in a sort of twenty-first century Silk Road. From South-east Asia to Eastern Europe and Africa, *Belt and Road* now includes seventy-one countries that account for half the world's population and a quarter of global GDP.

In short China will own the world's infrastructure, and as a consequence will control the world economy. To further fuel this, the pandemic has weakened western economies, such as Italy and some of the Eastern EU countries, who now seem only too keen to accept China's largesse. All this is aided, of course, by an America that has lost its soul and direction under an almost inconceivably psychotic and idiotic president. So, on a macro-level, will we emerge to a softer, cuddlier world? Well, if your idea of cuddly is picnicking with tanks in Tiananmen Square, maybe it just will.

And what of the micro perspective? What of the good things we have seen these last weeks: people acting collectively for the greater good, coming together to recognise the people in the front line of the fight, volunteering to look after each other in our communities? Well, there are lots of decent people around. We knew that. Most people, really. I'm inclined to go with Pareto, probably eighty per cent of people are decent - some more decent than others, of course, but most are basically decent nonetheless. But will this collective spirit, which underpins much of the more tangible manifestations of this decency. survive the crisis and walk out strongly into the new dawn? Well, we are going back to a world where many people's lives, jobs and wealth will have been destroyed. To a world where we are not only going into a recession, but are starting it with an unparallel amount of debt. To a world where our Health Service is so far behind in dealing with non-Covid illness that it is hard to see how it will catch up - even in the medium term. At the start of the lockdown there was a waiting list for operations of slightly more than four million - it is now closer to seven million. And hospitals going forward simply will not be able to be anything like as efficient as before, given the way they will have to adjust their processes to keep the virus at bay. Estimates for the efficiency drop vary from twenty per cent in London, where the conurbation means it is easier to separate out facilities as dedicated Covid centres, to fitty per cent in less populated areas of the country. In the longer term the pandemic might just be the exploding bomb which drives radical change in a healthcare system notoriously resistant to implementing change. But in the shorter term what we will have is a sicker population and worse healthcare. With more people out of work, higher taxes, and a less supported education system. Is this the backdrop for a caring, kinder world? A world focused on saving the planet? Sadly, I suspect not.

But, after all the doom and gloom, I shall end on a brighter note. In many ways this has been the great experiment; one we could never have hoped to plan. People have worked at home, by and large very successfully, and I think full and part-time home working will become the norm in the future - enhancing people's lives and, in many cases, make them happier and more productive in their jobs. As a byproduct, we will free up a massive amount of office space, which can be converted to meet our housing shortfall rather than trampling all over the green belt. Video conferencing is here to stay. I invested in two video conferencing suites five years ago - partly to have better, more personal conversations with clients than phone-calls, and partly to reduce the occasions our people travelled hundreds of miles in a day to attend meetings that only lasted an hour. They were an unmitigated failure. Our video suites are like the Carlsberg complaints office and the Everton trophy room - full of cobwebs and spiders. We will still never use them, but we now have the technology to make every call a 'facetime' call, and I for one think that makes the world a better place: more personal, less wasted time, less polluted. The internet has finally moved beyond porn as its raison d'être. And maybe, in time, we will have the potential for better, faster healthcare, as we are freed up to implement the kind of radical solutions that would never have got off the blocks in the past. I also believe that most of us have it in ourselves to achieve far more than we ever thought, but create our own personal myths which stop us from becoming the people we could be, and I would love to believe that this enforced detachment from the world will give many of us a better perspective on life, and that from that good things will emerge. So, there are shafts of sunlight through the rain. But I am a bit of dreamer, after all.

I started this essay talking of the worrying rise of China in world affairs, and moved on to a fairly depressing view of the landscape when we open the door to the world again, before trying to put some positive gloss on the whole thing. But what we really need, more than at any time in the last seventy-five years, is some genuine leadership. Someone who defines a vision that people believe in; which gives us collective hope. But now I really am dreaming.

1ST JUNE - GORDON IS A MORON

For me, as I work in splendid isolation, one of the more uplifting by-products of this lockdown period has been having the chance to reacquaint myself with some of the music of my past. Or rather semi splendid, semi-isolation - one of the prime motivations for listening to music non-stop being to drown out my sons' bickering, and their shouting down the internet at their friends as they play whatever bloody game it is that they play endlessly on their PS4s.

Anyhow, on this morning's stroll down musical memory lane, I was re-aquatinted with one of the great novelty records of all time: *Jilted John*, by Jilted John. Apart from being a cracking tune, this song has a particular memory for me, as a girl who lived on my floor at University actually used to go out with Jilted John. And did, indeed, jilt him. (She didn't literally live on my floor, you understand, but two rooms away on the same floor in Halls. But you get what I mean). I remember her telling me that she thought Graham was a bit of dick (his real name was Graham Fellows), but I seem to recall this opinion changing in direct relation to the success of his song, to the point that she massively regretted her impetuousness in dumping him when the song sky-rocketed to No 4 in the charts. Or 'Hit Parade' as we probably called it back then. I did try to persuade her that, if she hadn't jilted him, he wouldn't have gone on to be more spectacularly jilted by Julie, wouldn't have penned the song, wouldn't have become a pop star, and she would now be stuck with two kids in a Manchester council house with a dead-end boyfriend. And then she wouldn't have come to University and met such dazzling lights as me. I can't recall how well she received this. Not well, I suspect. I was still of the naïve view back then that you could persuade girls to sleep with you by the power of logic alone. Which was clearly nonsense, or else A J Ayer would not have followed up his masterpiece *Language, Truth and Logic*, with something so terminally dull as, *The Foundations of Empirical Knowledge*. His next rollercoaster would have been something far saucier, with much more tabloid appeal. *Using Paradoxes to Get Your Leg-Over*, maybe. Or, *Metaphysics and Epistemology: An Undergraduate's Guide to Logical Shagging*. Anyhow, I am clearly rambling here, so back to Jilted John. For those of you who don't know the song it begins:

I've been going out with a girl
Her name is Julie
But last night she said to me
When we were watching telly

(This is what she said)
She said listen John, I love you
But there's this bloke, I fancy
I don't want to two time you
So it's the end for you and me
Who's this bloke I asked her
Gordon, she replied
Not THAT puff, I said dismayed
Yes but he's no puff she cried

And then John goes on to serenade us with the fabulously catchy chorus:

But I know he's a moron, Gordon is a moron
Gordon is a moron, Gordon is a moron

Why am I sharing all this with you? Well as I said, I heard this for the first time in many years this morning, at almost exactly the time I was thinking, 'What morons', after reading a couple of news pieces from over the weekend. And so, without further prevarication, here are my two 'Gordons' from this morning's papers.

Gordon Number One is a complete idiot called Tim Matthews. Tim was that chap who reported Dominic Cummings for making a second trip up to Durham on April 19th - a claim strenuously denied by Cummings. Now, whatever you might think of Cummings, you probably wouldn't disagree that his alleged breaking of lockdown rules has been a massive distraction to the government at a time when we would much prefer that they be focused on the job in hand. His first trip up North - in my view, anyhow - was defensible on childcare grounds. But a second trip decidedly put him on thinner ice (I mean, who in their right mind would want to go that far North twice?) It turns out, however, that the smoking gun was a fake gun. Matthews had altered the figures on his running app to make it look like he had seen Mr. Cummings in Durham on April 1st - after the PM's aide had returned to London from his first trip. I could almost take this if he was some kind of leftie fanatic, but no - it was because Mr. Matthews apparently thinks himself something of the joker. 'I made that up afterwards, a few days ago in fact. I modified it for a little bit of comedy value.' Forgive me, Tim, if I don't get the joke. Much though I dislike Cummings, I would be quite happy to hold his coat whilst he did some equally hilarious things to you. Preferably with a brutally sharpened pencil - and one of Gwyneth Paltrow's vibrators strategically placed in your bottom for good measure.

The second Gordon is a woman - but she looks masculine enough to be a Gordon, so that's ok. Even before lockdown she sported a lockdown haircut, and a face that would make Gandhi want to give her a slap. Over the last three months the *National Education Union* has been head and shoulders above all others in their perpetration of seventies-reminiscent left-wing union nonsense. The secretary general of the NEU is Mary Bousted, a woman dedicated to her politics - and bugger the country at a time of crisis. And, it would seem, bugger the kids and their education and their future. Her name, amusingly, is an anagram for 'Used Bot', which seems an unlikely turn of events somehow. This weekend Mary dismissed the idea of schools making up for lost time during the summer holidays, saying her members had been working 'flat out' during lockdown and deserved a break. I'm not criticising teachers generally, as I am sure most of them have been doing their best in tough circumstances, but's its hardly the blitz spirit, is it Mary? Particularly when teachers get three times as much holiday as anyone else. She said that any headteachers looking to lay on catch-up classes, especially for those pupils going into GCSEs and A levels, should only offer voluntary clubs and activities during the school holidays. 'We don't think the emphasis should be on catch up because many of those children will need to re-socialise, and re-engage with a love of learning, and be involved in creative activities which enable them to become part of a wider society again, and have the desire to learn again.' she lectured, in the tone of someone who hasn't taught - or probably even seen - a child for the better part of twenty years. Quite how holiday clubs will foster a love of learning is a mystery. It strikes me that kids who are doing the GCSEs and 'A' levels next year just need to catch up. It also strikes me that Mary would be pretty pissed off if she couldn't have her routine facelift because all the nurses suddenly took six weeks off because they've been putting in a bit of a shift lately. So, Mary is Gordon Number Two. In fact, I take it back. She's Gordon Number One. Tim Matthews is just an idiot, whereas Mary is a dangerous, powerful idiot.

To celebrate my two Gordons, I will leave you with the words of the great Jilted John:

Oh, she's a slag and he's a creep
She's a tart, he's very cheap
She is a slut, he thinks he's tough
She is a bitch, he is a puff
Yeah yeah, it's not fair
Yeah yeah, it's not fair

Wise words mate. Wise words. No wonder my friend at University had the hots for you. Eventually.

5TH JUNE - GOOD GOLLY!

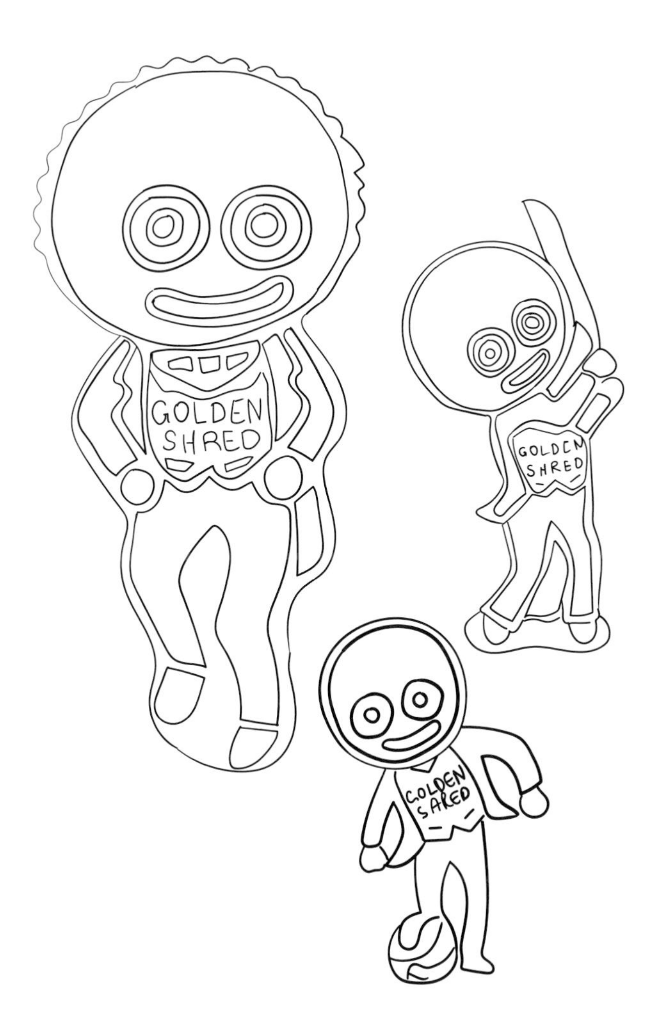

In my last journal I made the terrible mistake of quoting Jilted John from 1978:

She is a slut, he thinks he's tough
She is a bitch, he is a puff

This was clearly an appalling thing to have done. The word 'puff' has, quite rightly, been exorcised from all of our dictionaries - unless accompanied by either 'sugar', or, 'of wind', obviously. On behalf of Jilted John and *The Wuhan Diaries*, therefore, I apologise unreservedly for any offense it may have caused to anyone inside or outside of the LGBTUVWYZ community. I am, of course, in the process of resigning from all official posts and societies, fully accept your condemnation for this terrible oversight, and have put my name down for correctional training at the first available opportunity.

It did get me thinking, though, of words and symbols, and how these seem to have almost surpassed actions as the things people are most offended about in this woke world that we now live in. America is in turmoil following the George Floyd murder, and this has quite rightly sparked outrage around the world at a terrible crime, and served as a rallying point against discrimination generally - to a large part under the banner headline of 'Black Lives Matter'. A friend on Facebook (a non 'white' man) made a very interesting comment of this. He posted, 'It is the historic and continuing disproportionate and institutionalised bad treatment and inequality of one section of humanity that is the issue. Even the term 'racist' is a misnomer which helps fascists project their evil division and rhetoric. In reality there is only one race; the Human Race.' All of which I happen to agree with - it is actions, not labels, that are important. But, in this politically correct world we now inhabit, one could be forgiven for thinking that the opposite were true. Woe betide the person who uses yesterday's terminology for a describing a man's skin pigment, for instance - which is tough as the words one is sanctioned to use seem to change monthly. Now, it would appear, one is supposed to use the epithet 'person of colour', when it was not too long ago that people would get very hot under the collar indeed when described as being 'coloured' - which sounds remarkably similar to me. Moreover, where I the kind of chap to take offence easily, I could very well become offended by either of these on the basis I am being categorised, by inference, as being a person of 'no colour'. Which, apart from being quite an alarming concept, happens not to be true. I am not of no colour at all - indeed, after the recent warm spell, I can quite legitimately claim to be of a pretty similar colour to someone like, say - and I am plucking an example out of the air here - Meghan Markle.

Now, I get that Meghan has different ethnicity to me, as her mother was of African descent. And I get that she is, quite rightly, offended that her grandfather was forced to eat in the carpark of the KFC and not allowed in the store itself (though I do think she might have chosen a less stereotyped example of a black man in the Southern U.S. than one eating fried chicken). But she went on to say that, during her lifetime, 'Countless black jokes,' had been told in front of her, by people who were, 'unaware that I am the ethnically ambiguous fly on the wall.' In Meghan's mind, and in that of many of the liberal left, actions and words seem conflated, so that the two become one. I understand the logic of focusing on words, of course I do, and I can see that they can reinforce stereotypes. But what is really important is what someone means, and the unit of meaning is not the word, but the statement. Words acquire meaning in context, and this is where this fixation on the overwhelming importance of using politically right-on words breaks down, and actually becomes dangerous. Communication is, after all, a two-way process, and good communication is about both parties wanting to communicate - and understand - a shared message. It is not about the listener being pre-programmed to be offended because they choose to attribute meaning to words that are different to the way that the speaker intended them. If someone doesn't mean to cause offense, then surely, quite a lot of the time, does the responsibility for the offence not lie with the listener, who is choosing to be offended, rather than with the speaker?

Meghan was clearly uncomfortable about 'black' jokes. Now, I come from Liverpool, and I suspect there are at least as many scouse jokes as there are black jokes - few of which paint the inhabitants of my home town in a particularly admirable light. Some examples I've heard quite recently:

Give a scouser a fish, and he can eat for a day. Give him a fishing rod and he'll put it in your letterbox and nick your car keys.

My mate from Liverpool has started working in a local slaughterhouse, stunning the animals. They've never seen a scouser with a job.

What do you call a scouser in a suit? The accused.

I personally find them quite funny, even though they paint us Liverpudlians - including my family and friends - as feckless, lazy criminals. But I am pretty sure if I substituted the word 'scouser' with 'person of colour' I would cause no end of offense - and very possibly be accused of racial hatred. We should campaign for justice in society; we should strive to make the world a fair place, where people have equal opportunity and are not discriminated against on the base of race or colour. But do we not have a far better chance of achieving this if people choose to be offended by actions, by unfairness and prejudice, rather than simply by words? And we should be able to laugh at each other too? Because without laughter it's a pretty grey world - or should I more correctly say, 'world of little colour'?

I mentioned symbols earlier, and symbols are also important and can condition peoples' thinking. But equally, like words, symbols can be deliberately misinterpreted to construct offense where none was given. The Golly on the Roberson's jam-jar, for instance, is often seen as a quintessential symbol of white oppression over black people. The earliest mention of Golly, however, is as the hero in books of verse written by Bertha Upton in the 1890's, and illustrated by her daughter Florence. Mother and daughter created twelve books in all, featuring Golly as the central character who, with his friends the Dutch Dolls, had many fun adventures around the world. There wasn't a hint of 'racism' in these books - quite the reverse in fact, they showed black and white as equal and together. Golly then became best known in the 1920s, in the form of pin badges as the advertising logo for the *Robertson's Jam & Preserves Company*. The badges became so popular that other items of Golly advertising merchandise became available, and each year brought new items for kids to add to their collections. It is less well-known that all the monies raised from sales of this merchandise were donated to the various charities that Robertson's supported. These included *Cancer Research, Cystic Fibrosis, The Royal National Lifeboat Institution and Leukaemia Research*. Robertson's also used the Golly badges and merchandise to support several other worthwhile causes, including the *Viota Scheme* (promoting healthy eating and baking), road safety, and promoting recycling. Eventually though, Golly perished at the hands of the PC brigade, who continually equated Golly to the word 'Golliwog'. It is believed that Robertson's were so taken aback that anybody could even think their company brand stood for racist views that they didn't even attempt to defend their position, but instead chose to retire Golly, even though several surveys supported the view that Robertson's should ignore the dissenters and continue to use their Golly logo.

So, one of the greatest ever corporate supporters of charities, which stood for healthy eating, recycling and our children's safety, was finally seen off in the name of racism because Golly's face was the wrong colour, and people continually misconstrued his name as Golliwog. It makes you think doesn't it?

9TH JUNE - ANOTHER ROLE OF HAZARD TAPE, SIR?

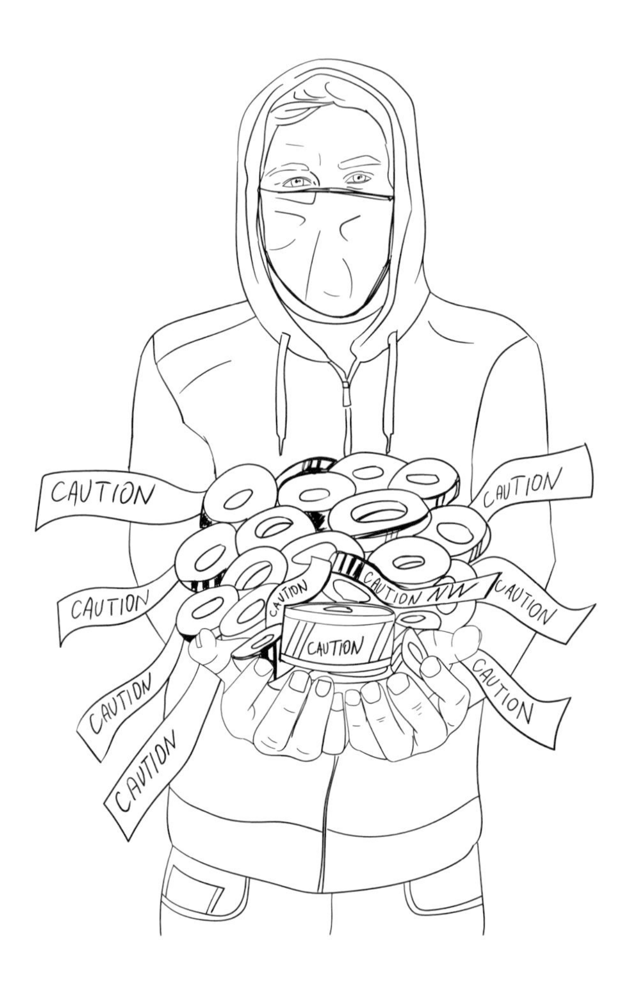

When I first went to senior school, there was a rule that boys travelling to and from school had to wear their caps at all times. But only the boys in the first two years. For us eleven and twelve-year old lads this was a howling injustice. It seemed to have no logic whatsoever, but existed merely to embarrass us. As you might imagine, on more than one occasion I was spotted capless by an eagle-eyed teacher, and ended up with lines or detention as a punishment. Now, I know not everybody is the same, and particularly when they are in difficult or scary situations, many people want to grab hold of rules as their lifejacket to buffer them against troubled waters. But for others, thinking that those rules are unnecessary, or contradictory, is liable to make them ignore them completely. And for others still, rules are always just there to be broken, and they have no consideration for others or the impact of their actions generally. Think, 'People who throw their McDonald's wrapper out of their car windows', for this group. Or, 'Complete bastards', as I like to call them.

Now, when we went into lockdown, we immediately had a bunch of rules to which we were told to conform. And, by and large, the government very successfully persuaded us to comply with these rules under the mantra of: 'Stay at home. Protect the NHS. Save Lives'. It was one big rule really, with a couple of bits tagged on the side about exercise and key workers, so it was relatively easy to enforce and understand. But even then, lots of people got their knickers in a complete twist over interpretation - where I live, whether people were allowed to work on their allotments or not was a question which gave rise to major consternation. Some people just seem to find it easier to have a hard and fast rule rather than trust themselves to use their intelligence and judgement. In any event, the government clearly didn't want people exercising judgement at that time. They just wanted people to stay at home. And against a backdrop of an escalating body count the government were, to a large extent, supported by the populace and seen to be doing the right thing. But now we are trying to get out of lockdown, this whole rule thing is becoming a complete mess. It is hard to not come to the conclusion that we are making rules for the sake of rules right now, and that our approach is so deep-rooted in the belief that we are all eleven-year old children who need to be made to wear our caps that good sense is being strangled in a mountain of hazard tape and floor markings.

The best way to eliminate coronavirus in the UK, of course, would be to stop anyone coming into the country ever again, and to keep ourselves shut up in our houses until we haven't had a single case of Covid-19 for months. There are a couple of minor problems here of course: the country will go bankrupt, lots of people will get sick with other ailments and not be treated, and the rest of us will go stark-staring mad. So, clearly, we need to try and find the right balance - between opening up the country again and not doing this in a way that will cause the disease to get a second wind and give us a bloody nose. And our way of doing this has been to make a whole set of new rules which gradually moderate the one big rule that we started with. The problem though, is that some of these rules are just plain stupid, and people can see this. I can't imagine there is anyone in the country who actually sees the logic of keeping our air travel open to the whole world while they were infected, but then effectively closing it down now that they are not. Or who thought it was a good idea to allow everyone to pop on the tube to work, but not go and sit in their mum's back garden for half an hour on the way home.

Boris was roundly chastised for his speech telling us to, 'stay alert'. Many, who one would have had down as being quite intelligent, were ridiculing him on the basis that people can't 'be alert' for something they can't see, smell or taste. Which is, frankly, nonsense; of course you can. If people understand what we are trying to achieve, and how, then they can be very much on the alert as to whether they are doing the right things to help achieve it. I read an interesting article about the approach in Portugal this morning. There, the emphasis seems to be less on setting rules, and more on engendering understanding, so people act proportionately and with common sense. In Lisbon airport, for instance, there aren't miles of hazard tape, and it's possible for a family of four to remain self-contained and sit in a row of four seats because the two in the middle have not been taped off. Where different households come together, people simply know to leave an empty seat or two between them. Rather than buy up the world's stock of hazard tape, Portugal has more wisely invested in hand sanitizer and face masks. The overriding principle guiding the lifting of their lockdown- which the Portuguese seem to understand - is that the transmission of droplets from one household to another should be avoided. It's a very simple principle, but if people get this then there is a very good chance they will behave wisely - through desire, and through peer pressure too I suspect. In other words, help people to act responsibly, rather than treat them as idiots, and there is a decent chance that we will actually achieve far more.

Apparently, every shop, bar and restaurant in Portugal has a bottle of hand sanitiser at the entrance; you simply don't get in without first cleaning your hands. It takes only a moment, and is the most effective public health intervention we have. Many bars and restaurants have a bottle on every table. Then there are face masks. We appear to have completely contradictory views on this in the UK. *Public Health England* tells us the virus is held in droplets that emerge from our mouths and noses. They warn us to cover our faces if we cough or sneeze lest we spread them to others or surfaces around us. They say we should stand two metres from someone we are talking to in order to prevent droplets passing between us. And yet the same organisation maintains, throughout its 'Covid-secure' guidelines for business, that face-coverings are only 'marginally beneficial', while at the same time mandating their use for doctors, nurses, carers, hospital visitors and public transport passengers. They either do some good or they don't - you can't have it both ways PHE! In Portugal they seem to have jumped on the 'does some good' side of the fence. The etiquette here is that they should be worn, not outside (where the danger of transmission is massively reduced), but whenever you enter a business or a crowed space. In a restaurant or bar, you enter wearing a mask but remove it while sitting down to eat or drink. If you get up to go to the loo you put it on again as a courtesy to those you pass on the way. This all sounds jolly sensible to me. You explain properly to people how the virus is transmitted - and the likelihood of it being transmitted in different scenarios - and provide some basic rules and the infrastructure to enable the population at large to be sensible. Will everyone be one hundred per cent sensible? Of course not. Do we need ways to encourage people to continue to 'stay alert'? Probably. Is it better than making us all wear our caps on the way to school? Almost certainly.

16TH JUNE - BE THE CHANGE THAT YOU WISH TO SEE IN THE WORLD

Victor Hugo said it best: 'Nothing is more powerful than an idea whose time has come.' And the 'Black Lives Matter' movement is an idea whose time certainly appears to have arrived. Without question, the pandemic has been the kindling which has nurtured the BLM flame, and in a world that had changed and seemed to almost stop overnight, where people were both scared and thoughtful, the image of a handcuffed man having someone kneel on his neck for eight minutes captured attention in a way that simply wouldn't have happened a few months ago. It is an image that has triggered a worldwide reaction - and lockdown has provided the wind to spread the flame of a cause, with people both horrified, and, at the same time, desperate to have a justifiable reason to get outside and start feeling like they are alive again.

Civil Rights have always bubbled somewhere near the surface in my lifetime. I am just about old enough to be touched by Martin Luther King. I remember seeing his 'I have a dream' speech on TV - I was only five years old, and my memory is less of the speech than of the effect it had on my parents, but it seemed both important and unsettling at the same time. My early adulthood was lived against the backdrop of the struggle against Apartheid in South Africa. So, in some ways, there is nothing new in this BLM thing today. Certainly, there is nothing new in the eternal struggle of people seeking to create fairness and justice in and unfair and unjust world. And it is hard not to be behind this, to believe in giving people - the world over - the opportunities to live good, happy and productive lives. To believe in the same justice for all, in fairness, and in not discriminating against anyone on the base of their race or colour. But all of that doesn't mean that I don't find much of the narrative around this BLM movement to be pretty bloody irritating.

There is a moment in an *Only Fools and Horses* episode, where all the main characters are in the pub, talking about people who have had their Andy Warhol 'five minutes of fame'. Rodney mentions Rene and Renate and Simon Dee, before Trigger pops up and says, 'Gandhi.' When they all look a bit mystified, he explains that, 'He only made one movie, and then we never saw him again.' A brilliant line from one of my favourite TV characters of all time. And it allows me to lighten the mood a bit as well give a nice segue to Gandhi. You see, Gandhi happens to be one of my favourite real characters of all time. I don't wish that to sound as pretentious as it does, but he is. A man of great intelligence and insight, which he combined with incredible physical bravery. He had the ability to communicate brilliantly, not with oratorical fireworks, but with the simple integrity of his words. A man who changed the world by reason rather than anger, by humanity rather than prejudice.

Like many of you, the BLM movement has made me question some of my thinking and motivations about race and racism. But, equally, it has also made me question the motivations and actions of a vast number of people who seem very keen on self-flagellation, who are looking to foster a climate of guilt and anger, and to blanketly criticise and belittle many of the good things about our country and our society. Faced with some conflict of how I feel about all of this, I thought it might be helpful to pull on some of the thoughts of Mahatma Gandhi, who clearly has a whole lot more experience and insight than me in these matters, and help these guide my thinking.

'Our ability to reach unity in diversity will be the beauty and the test of our civilisation.'

One of the things that disturbs me about a large proportion (but not all, admittedly) of the BLM movement is the use of language that encourages division rather than unity. I object fundamentally to the constant changing of the way in which I have to refer to people, and the assumption that I am racist if I don't abide by today's rules. 'A person of colour', in my view, is offensive and divisive. I have a colour; I'm not bloody transparent after all! Whilst I understand the need for people who are treated badly, as a consequence of their colour, to band together to create a collective force for change, what I don't understand is why I should be made to feel like a morally lesser being because I don't meet the ethnic criteria for their club.

'A man is but the product of his thoughts. What he thinks, he becomes.'

I was watching footage of one of the demonstrations in England. I'm not sure which one, but my attention was drawn to a placard being carried by a white bloke. It read, simply, 'I'm sorry'. For some reason this infuriated me. He may well have been apologising personally for some terrible racist wrong he had committed in his past, but I am guessing this wasn't what was going on. He was, I suspect. the racially 'woke' white man apologising on behalf of all of us for white oppression. Well, here's a thought, black people do shit too. Not least of which are the black-on-black crimes of much modern-day slavery in Africa - the very crimes that whites are accused of in the (now quite distant) past. There are lovely white people, and there are horrible white people; lovely black people, and horrible black people. No one group owns all the sins or all the moral high ground. As Gandhi said, a man is indeed the product of his thoughts, and if we are unable to see the good things that we achieved as a country - as well as the bad things - we will become a group of people who sees itself as inferior and guilty. Everything black is good; everything white bad. And that's neither true nor helpful.

'I will not let anyone walk through my mind with their dirty feet.'

A couple of days back, I read of an incident involving Leona Lewis. She was apparently in some kind of antique shop in Chelsea with her father, where they were the only non-white people in the shop. The owner was, apparently, keeping a suspicious eye on the two of them, and became quite rude as she suspected they were there to steal some stuff rather than fork-out the readies. Leona took offence to this - which I completely understand - and made a bit of a scene. Good on her in my book. When she kicked-off, however, apparently most of the other people in the shop walked out, and in the telling of the tale Leona castigated them for not standing up for her and arguing against the injustice. Her view seemed to be that, because they didn't choose to man her barricades, this proved that they were inherently racist - the 'silence is violence' line in thinking. Well, we English tend not to like confrontation, and will often go quite a long way to avoid it. I wasn't there, but I suspect this was what was actually going on for most of the people who left. They just didn't want to get involved in a fight - about anything - when they had only popped out to look at some silver Victorian napkin holders. But this supposition, that people are racist unless they say and do exactly what is demanded of them, is wrong. One of the great things about the freedom that we enjoy is that we are free to have our own thoughts and ideas, our own idiosyncrasies, cowardices and contradictions. It is what makes this an infinitely better place to live than, say, China or Russia. Any movement that seeks to control and judge what people think, which seeks to force compliance with their view rather than persuade people to agree freely, is as wrong as the things they are seeking to change. Change my mind by all means, but do not seek to walk over it with your dirty feet.

'Hate the sin, love the sinner.'

Much of the BLM activity seems to have centred around eliminating symbols of past injustice, and in particular statues to people who are deemed to be 'racist'. The narrative here (and I hate that word, even though I've used it twice so far) is that we need to exorcise from history people who perpetrated the slave trade two hundred or more years ago, or indeed anything of a vaguely colonial bent - irrespective of whatever good things they might have done. I have two problems with this. The first is that, in order to not recreate the sins of history, we need to embrace it. Far better, in my view, to let the statues stand, and see them as lessons to be learnt from, rather than tear them down in a Stalinist fit of anger and retribution. The second is that we are all flawed. 'Let he who is without sin cast the first stone.' as Jesus said. So, is it right we want a world where the bad somebody does completely eclipses the good of that same person? Take Cecil Rhodes, for instance. Much is made of his exploitation of black labour in Africa - and I am a long way from saying that I think he was an all in all good chap - but consider this quote from a speech made by him, at the tender age of twenty-four, in a mining town in Kimberley, South Africa:

'The object of which I intend to devote my life is the defence and extension of the British Empire. I think that object a worthy one because the British Empire stands for the protection of all the inhabitants of a country in life, liberty, property, fair play and happiness, and it is the greatest platform the world has ever seen for these purposes and for human enjoyment.'

These are not the words of a one-dimensional villain, but of a man of belief who did things which, with the benefit of looking back from today's perspective, were wrong. The end does not justify the means, of course it doesn't, but Rhodes achieved great things, and became a great philanthropist to provide some balance to the way we should look at him. Those who want to pull down Rhodes' statue, and erect one to Floyd George - a man convicted of armed robbery of a private house - might want to dwell on this.

'If I had no sense of humour, I would long ago have committed suicide.'

Ricky Gervais made a great comment last year:

'Please stop saying, 'You can't joke about anything anymore.' You can. You can joke about whatever the fuck you like. And some people won't like it and they will tell you they don't like it. And then it's up to you whether you give a fuck or not. It's a good system.'

I think Gandhi would have liked that. We have moved into a world where any humour involving a stereotype of any racial characteristic is deemed unacceptable and racist. Apart from being pretty bloody miserable as a way to live, this just seems wrong. Without wishing to harp back to my youth again, I grew up with Alf Garnett as the bigot in *Till Death Us Do Part*. It was Alf's racist rants that made many who watched confront bigotry for the first time, and achieved more than a thousand well-intentioned liberal politicians have ever done with their seriousness. We're not allowed to watch him now, of course, as its deemed offensive. For me, if I were to get chatting to a black guy in the pub, I would like to be able to think that most jokes are not off-limits, and for him to think the same about me. Personally, I wouldn't take offence at jokes which cast my scouse 'community' as robbing, work-shy wasters. I get that there is a limit, but people who can laugh together, bond together. Friendships form, and understanding and caring are fostered. Of course there is an 'offense' line that can be crossed - words and ideas do matter - but people who want to be offended, who want their own prejudices confirmed, set that line in a very different place to people who simply want to be able to laugh about life, and about the differences that define us.

'Poverty is the worst form of violence.'

If we look at the UK, much is being made of the statistic that BAME people are more at risk of COVID than non-BAME people, between twenty per cent and fifty per cent now seems to be the suggested uplift. The dialogue for the reasons for this now seems to revolve around 'structural racism', with the narrative that our society deliberately disadvantages these ethnic groupings, leaving them exposed to the ravages of the virus in a way 'privileged' white people are not. Now, I can well imagine that the less affluent in society are more vulnerable - they probably have worse diet, live in closer proximity to more people, have more underlying health conditions than people who live in wealthier areas. But not all of the people in this situation are 'black'. The worst sufferers in the UK are people with Bangladeshi heritage, who have twice the risk apparently. But we don't hear much of them. Or of comparators to white people who live in equally poor conditions. Poverty and lack of opportunity are not just a 'black' problem, and the people seeking to treat it as such are as guilty of racism as the people they vilify. As Gandhi once said, 'I believe in equality for everyone, except reporters and photographers.'

17TH JUNE - THE END OF THE LINE

I began this diary on 22nd March - the day before the government officially put the lockdown in place. Almost three months have passed since then, and you would be hard pushed to find someone who wouldn't see this as an unforgettable and seismic time in our history. The world changed overnight; for a while it almost seemed as though it had stopped to allow us off for a brief respite. We are not yet back to normal - nowhere near it - but, for the time being at least, we can see some light at the end of the tunnel. Just before the lockdown I took my son, Anthony, to see Liverpool play Atletico Madrid - an infamous game, that should never have been allowed to go ahead, and to which a great many Covid-related deaths have been directly attributed. This was the last game Liverpool played. Football, albeit an odd fan-less version of the game, starts again tonight, and Liverpool play their first game of the resumption against Everton on Sunday. For me, the return to watching my beloved Reds is the first big symbol of a return to some inkling of normality, and as such this seems as good a moment as any to hang up my *Wuhan Diaries*' pen. For some reason having these two Liverpool games act as the bookends to my diary seems appropriate somehow.

I started the Diaries partly to give me something to do (other than watch re-runs of *Cheers* and worry about whether I could afford to pay the staff), and partly because I didn't want this time to just blend together into a single blur. I wanted some personal record of this momentous and historic moment in our lives - and to have something concrete, too, to give my boys so their memory is of something more than us all being locked-up and annoying each other for months on end, with each day being much like the last. I had a skim back over everything I have written last night, and hopefully it has achieved this in a small way. Amazingly, it is now sixty-five thousand words, so I will pull it together into a book sometime soon. So, that will be two books I have written that none of my three sons will ever finish!

If you have followed my posts on Facebook, thank you - even if you only read occasionally, that is gratifying. I hope you found my daily rants at least a tiny bit entertaining. Stay aware, and in the words of Maria von Trapp in the Sound of Music, 'So long, farewell, auf Wiedersehen, goodbye.'

Thank you for reading my diary. We are now out of lockdown, though not out of the virus' firing line just yet; we are also trying to pick ourselves up from the damage done to our health system and to the economy. So I hope you found my book a useful diversion in these strange times - to be a tiny bit thought-provoking, and hopefully made you smile a few times along the way. If so, then writing it was worthwhile. And if it did, I would really love it if you could spare a moment to leave a review on *Amazon*. If you didn't, don't. Obviously. But don't let that stop you from buying *Cycling Down the Street*, which I just know you will absolutely love.